Straw for the Br

Straw for the Bricks

Theological Reflection in Practice

Gary O'Neill (editor)
and
Liz Shercliff

scm press

© The Contributors 2018

Published in 2018 by SCM Press
Editorial office
3rd Floor, Invicta House,
108–114 Golden Lane,
London EC1Y 0TG, UK
www.scmpress.co.uk

SCM Press is an imprint of Hymns Ancient & Modern Ltd (a registered charity)

Hymns Ancient & Modern® is a registered trademark of
Hymns Ancient & Modern Ltd
13A Hellesdon Park Road, Norwich,
Norfolk NR6 5DR, UK

The author and publisher gratefully acknowledge permission to
use the following copyright material:

David Coghlan and Teresa Brannick, *Doing Action Research in Your Own Organization*,
4th edn, text quotation (p. 123) copyright © 2014 by David Coghlan and Teresa Brannick.
Reprinted by permission of SAGE Publications, Ltd.

Patricia O'Connell Killen and John De Beer, *The Art of Theological Reflection*,
Crossroad Publishing. Illustrations 'Enter into the Experience' (p. 22) and 'Prism of
Experience' (p. 60) copyright © 1994 by the illustrator Kathleen M. Sievers.
Used by permission of the illustrator.

Scripture quotations are from the New Revised Standard Version of the Bible, Anglicized
Edition, copyright 1989, 1995 by the Division of Christian Education of the National
Council of the Churches of Christ in the USA. Used by permission. All rights reserved.

And from the Authorized Version of the Bible (The King James Bible), the rights in
which are vested in the Crown, are reproduced by permission of the Crown's Patentee,
Cambridge University Press.

British Library Cataloguing in Publication data

A catalogue record for this book is available
from the British Library

978 0 334 05500 6

Typeset by Regent Typesetting Ltd
Printed and bound by
CPI Group (UK) Ltd

Contents

List of Figures and Tables

Figures

Tables

Preface

Personal acknowledgements from Gary O'Neill

My thanks go to all in the Education for Ministry (EfM) community with whom I have had the privilege of being companions on the Way, and all mentors and trainers who, through their generous endurance of events I have facilitated, have contributed to my practice. During the research which contributed to this work many people have supported or assisted me and among them I particularly thank:

- Professor Elaine Graham, MProf supervisor, and my peer researchers on the DProf programme, especially Andy Wier, Alastair Prince, Edmund Betts, Katja Stuerzenhofecker, Stephen Tranter and Tony Whelan, for their continued presence, criticism and constant humour.
- My colleagues at All Saints Centre for Mission and Ministry, who have formed the theological reflection team of tutors over the last decade: Andrew Rudd, Anne Davidson-Lund, Beverley Angier, Caroline Hewitt, Christopher Halliday, David Lesley, David Sharples, Heather Carty, Jo Parker, Judith Evans, Liz Shercliff.
- The international directors of EfM: Catherine Hall, Karen Meridith, Peter Williams and Trevor Smith for encouragement and personal hospitality.
- All the members of the international co-operative inquiry groups: Adele Sinclair, Alec Clark, Ann Dittmar-McCollim, Art Martens, Barbara Booth, Betty Revelant, Bill Colbrahams, Catherine Hall, Christopher Halliday, Denise Ferguson, Frank Nelson, Gary Harch, Helen Malcolm, Helen Wilderspin, Jan Craft, Jane McCraw, Jane Mitchell, Joanna Hobart, Judith Wigglesworth, Karen Meridith, Kevin Bourke, Lindy Driver, Lois Weise, Lorraine Dawson, Lynelle Osburn, Lynne Cain, Margaret M, Michael Richards, Noel Workman, Norma Anderson, Peter Williams, Rachel Browning, Rachel Martin, Roger Cooper, Roger Sharr, Sr Maureen CSF, Steve Hallmark, Sue Beauclerc, Trevor Smith, Tricia Carter, Victoria Heenan.
- Three friends who stood outside the research project and commented on my early drafts: Ann Philips, Patricia O'Connell Killen, and David

Goodbourn, who sadly died without seeing the final draft – a loss to his family, friends and the world of practical theology.

Personal acknowledgements from Liz Shercliff

My work in this volume stems from my own experience as a preacher and teacher of homiletics. This experience has been supported and encouraged by many – not least my ever-patient husband, Dave Shercliff, who faithfully listens to my sermons as they gestate.

I would also like to thank:

- The Revd Canon Dr Christopher Burkett, who has consistently encouraged me to develop my homiletic practice and share it in print as a regular columnist in *The Preacher* magazine.
- The Revd Dr Kate Bruce for encouraging me to believe that we should not write or speak about preaching without including our own sermons.
- Dr Katja Stuerzenhofecker who proposed to me that my work on preaching is at least as much a calling as an academic contribution.
- The many students who have not only listened to my ideas but engaged with them and developed them further.

Introduction

'*Quintessentially an experiential activity*' is a phrase coined by Judith Thompson, Stephen Pattison and Ross Thompson to describe theological reflection (2008, 2), which is why this book is rooted in the experience of its authors. The publication of a handbook for theological reflection using our version of the four-source model is a distillation of decades of practical experience rooted in six major areas: i) the work of Patricia O'Connell Killen and John de Beer's *The Art of Theological Reflection* (1994); ii) the Education for Ministry[1] Programme internationally; iii) the Exploring faith Matters[2] community in the UK; iv) the learning community All Saints Centre for Mission and Ministry[3]; v) the research areas of the primary authors; and vi) their ministerial practice.

Gary O'Neill on 'Why Straw for the Bricks'?

I have been actively involved in the practice of theological reflection for more than 20 years. I am not a journaler or diarist by nature and yet I can recall vividly many of the reflections I have participated in. This way of making sense of my experience has always seemed natural and I know it has shaped my life. Here are three examples.

In the mid-1990s, in my first theological reflection group in a North Manchester suburb, a young woman rooted a reflection on her experience as a crossing patrol officer[4] whose responsibility was to see schoolchildren across the road. I recall strong feelings on her part about adults who ignored the crossing staffed by this woman and instead chose, with her in view (and of the children whom she guided over the road), to cross the road away from the patrol point. Her conviction was that this set a poor example to children and that a responsible adult would always use a crossing patrol point, thereby offering a powerful and influential role model for children. This reflection had engaged with Scripture, and as an ordained person, a 'professional', I was hearing God speak through an ordinary person. I changed my behaviour.

Ten years later I was in the picturesque coastal setting of South Devon participating in a reflection with my Birmingham city centre group, undertaken out of doors on a sunny afternoon. The conversation was around life-threatening or near-fatal experiences. I can still picture a woman and a man standing on plastic garden chairs debating, surrounded by the rest of the group involved in the conversation. The moment was rich with emotion, passion, energy and intellectual rigour. Within a year, the man had died, but his contribution to that reflection, the ongoing life of the group, and his final months in hospital, brought home to me the fragility and beauty of created life together with the wonder of looking life and death in the face. This spoke theologically of what it means to be fully human and alive in a fleeting world.

In 2011 I spent several days in an Oxford retreat house with a group of friends. In a series of conversations, we imagined scenes where the grass appeared greener on the other side of the fence, and what it felt like to be in a fenced and gated field, however pleasant the meadow experience might be. In listening to one person's experience of what it is like to be constrained by the health needs of a loved one, I was able to explore feelings I had of being restricted by the combination of my employment and a large mortgage on a new home. Theologically we were exploring the discipline of limiting oneself and the nature of a God who can or cannot limit Godself.

In all three of these stories there are significant theological themes and yet they were deliberately ordinary, emphasizing the everyday usefulness of reflection such as this.

To me this kind of reflection – which I deem to be theological because in practising it I acknowledge the reality of God – has always seemed accessible. However, in the field of practical theology, despite the assertion by some that theological reflection is the glue that holds the whole discipline together, many practitioners bemoan the lack of skill and ability of individuals and groups to engage in serious theological reflection (e.g. Pattison, Thompson and Green (2003, 129); Thompson, Pattison and Thompson (2008, viii); and Smith (2008, 31)). People apparently lack the resources to do so and are like the Hebrew slaves of Exodus 5.7 being asked to make *straw without bricks*.

My aim over the last ten years has been to hone and refine a 'four-source' model of theological reflection as a credible alternative to the current preference for the use of the pastoral cycle in the UK and to offer co-operative inquiry as an appropriate research methodology for practical theology. This combination of action research method and theological reflection model directly challenges a recent fashion for regarding all research in practical theology as action research – despite the degree of anonymity frequently practised – since it will of necessity expose myself and my practice as a facilitator to the reader. However that process pans out, I believe it will usher in *better-quality straw for the bricks*.

This is not a book that necessarily demands to be read straight through or in any particular order; the reader will be naturally drawn to the chapters that interest them. Chapter 1 'Introducing the model' gives a basic introduction to the four-source model and will be useful for those who come to this book with little knowledge or understanding of its use or provenance. Chapter 2 'Researching the model' retells the story of how I, together with many others, birthed a method of research rooted in action research, using co-operative inquiry groups. Those who are interested in the practicalities of an action research project within the field of practical theology might start here. For those who already have significant experience in the use of the four-source model will hopefully find waiting for them in Chapter 3 'Using the basic model in practice' a new manual for using the model, since nothing so detailed has appeared in the public domain for over 20 years. Finally, Chapter 4 'Developing skills and understanding' will be of interest to adult educators, those who train facilitators or mentors in theological reflection, and anyone seeking to wish to hone their existing skills.

For the last decade, I have been the Director of Exploring faith Matters in the UK. I have an MA in Adult Education with Theological Reflection and an MProf, obtained from the Professional Doctorate Programme at the University of Chester, through which Liz Shercliff is currently researching, and used as a springboard for the Women's Voices series of annual conferences.

Liz Shercliff on theological reflection in practice

Theological reflection, rather like preaching, should be both disclosive and prophetic (Walton, 2014, 9). Disclosive, in that it reveals the meanings and beliefs behind what we do and say. Prophetic, in that it disturbs and challenges accepted norms. In terms both of preaching and Bible reading (personally and in teaching), I have found theological reflection based on the four-source model expounded here to be a useful tool.

I began to explore the use of theological reflection as a tool for sermon preparation as a result of having read and marked around 500 sermons submitted by students training for authorized ministry. Despite variations in quality, overall they seemed generic and distant. The same sermon could have been preached by almost anyone, anytime and anywhere. The predominant use of the historical-critical method of exegesis distanced the reader/preacher from the text and never successfully re-joined them, so that biblical passages seemed to be drained of life by the process. Reading biblical passages in the context of theological reflection, by contrast, brought the Bible to life, enabling it to speak today. As can be seen in my subsequent chapters, I have encouraged the use of reflection in sermon preparation to make present the person of the speaker and the voice of the congregation.

My chapters contain substantial excerpts from sermons. This reflects the importance I attach to preaching, rather than any claim to personal excellence in preaching. I am a practical theologian and, as such, seek practical outcomes from my work. My hope in theological reflection, exegesis and preaching is always that the text might live.

I have aimed to illustrate the use of theological reflection as a tool for sermon preparation and for teaching both homiletics and exegesis. In my experience it has released my students and my text from the shackles of historical-critical readings, and opened Scripture so that more voices might be heard.

In Chapter 7 'Reflective preaching', I explore my own role as the preacher (position and experience), the part played by the congregation (culture), and how we read the biblical text (tradition). In Chapter 5 'Teaching biblical studies' we consider how experience might position students in relation to biblical texts and ways to help them appreciate this. We then move on to classroom practices. Chapter 6 'Theological reflection and exegesis' explores, using examples, how each source might help readers to reflect on New Testament passages. Chapter 8 'Using group theological reflection to prepare sermons' is simply a report of what happened when two tutors worked with a group using theological reflection to prepare a sermon. The outcomes of the reflection and both sermons are included. My four chapters are driven by the 'so what' of practical theology – if theological reflection is a worthwhile practice, how might it work out in preaching, teaching and reading the Bible?

Gary O'Neill on other contributors

In Liz's Chapter 8 the colleague she is working with is Robin Pye – a parish priest who teaches preaching in Chester Diocese. He has used theological reflection in both his teaching and parochial ministry.

After Liz Shercliff's four chapters on practice there are a further two contributors, both of whom have been part of the team of staff teaching theological reflection at All Saints over the last few years.

In Chapter 9 'Poetry' Andrew Rudd explores the connections between the way poetry works and the use of an image in the four-source model. Andrew Rudd is a spiritual director and Reader in the Church of England, frequently leading retreats and quiet days. Since Autumn 2017 he has been poet in residence at Manchester Cathedral. He has retired from his work as a lecturer in Education and Creative Writing, but teaches ordinands and trainee readers for the All Saints formation programme. Andrew has a PhD in Poetry and Spirituality, and his poetry is widely published.

In Chapter 10 'Theological reflection as praxis' Judith Evans recounts how she successfully employed a basic version of the four-source model in a parochial setting to enable a fruitful discussion on what was potentially a divisive issue, that of re-marriage. Those who are part of a ministry team in a parish or church may find this interesting because at the time the exploration took place she was a licensed Reader in the Church of England, and not therefore the head of the ministry team or chair of the church's Parochial Church Council; a good example of shared ministry. Judith is currently completing her Masters in Contextual and Practical Theology.

In Chapter 11 'Theological action research' I offer a contribution to the debate within practical theology on the nature of action research within that field, before adding some 'Final thoughts' in Chapter 12.

Editor's note

The reader may be puzzled over the childlike quality of some of the illustrations offered in this book; they are reduced photographs of what was *actually* drawn in a reflection. None of the participants is a skilled artist and accurate representation is not what is sought. However, the sketches are often profound in that they capture in a few strokes the essence of the world being explored and offer opportunities both for members of the group to confirm with each other the nature of the world they are exploring and to encourage the use of the imagination.

Notes

1 EfM, or Education for Ministry, is a long-distance learning programme established by the University of the South, Sewanee, Tennessee, USA. EfM groups consist of 6–12 students with a mentor whose task is to facilitate learning rather than teach. Each mentor is accredited by the programme and undertakes regular training. www.efm.sewanee.edu

2 A sister of the EfM programme, 'Exploring faith Matters' in the UK is a dispersed network community dedicated to the development of adult discipleship. At the heart of its life are theological conversation groups. www.efm.org.uk

3 All Saints is a Church of England training institution based in the North West serving six diocese and training candidates for licensed and ordained ministry. It is part of the 'Common Awards' programme accredited by Durham University at both undergraduate and postgraduate level. www.allsaintscentre.org

4 She actually said 'lollipop lady'.

PART ONE

Straw for the Bricks

Introducing the model

GARY O'NEILL

Just before lunch on an induction day for new students at All Saints, everyone gathers in a small hall, in which space has been created to wander around, and a member of staff outlines what will happen over the next 45 minutes. The students are invited to watch a short slide show of photographs of homeless people in and around the streets of Manchester – the images are accompanied by Ralph McTell's 1969 song 'Streets of London', but no commentary is offered. When the short presentation concludes the students are asked to respond to what they see and feel, by wandering around the hall via each of its four corners, in any order they choose. In each corner there is a member of staff and large self-stick sheets of paper, together with large pens, on which to write responses. In one corner they are invited to share what they think Scripture has to say about homelessness or poverty. In a second corner they are invited to think about how the way the world we live in comments on homelessness: what, for example, would a *Daily Mail* headline say about homeless people; what would the *Guardian* comment; how would your favourite radio host deal with the issue? In a third corner people are gently invited, if they wish, to share their personal experience of homeless people or homelessness. In a fourth corner the participants are asked to discern what their instinctive or emotive reaction is to homelessness; it is explained that they do not have to justify or defend what they might vocalize.

It is suggested that when they have visited each corner once, they do so again to hear or read what other people are saying and join in the conversation there if they wish. Finally, they are encouraged to mingle in the centre of the room and share with each other their experience of the last 30 minutes or so. Instructions given, the music starts, and 18 pictures drift across the large screen at one side of the hall – some people remain standing to watch.

The exercise is ended after about 40 minutes by the same member of staff who offered the original invitation. 'What we have just shared in together is what life is like at All Saints – together as staff and students we are a learning community. We all bring our extensive personal experience to the process of ministerial formation; some of us feel very strongly about certain issues; together we study the Scriptures alongside the Church's ongoing response; and we are aware that we live in a specific time and place in a country with its own customs and practices. Now it is time for lunch!'

The exercise always creates a buzz among the students; presenting an opportunity to physically move about at will, choosing with whom to interact, and providing an excuse for people to talk with those to whom they have not previously spoken.

At no point is the phrase 'theological reflection' used. At no point is the four-source model mentioned. At no point are the sources of that model named: Tradition (the Judeo-Christian tradition); Culture (the world we live in); Experience (my personal experience); or Position (visceral or gut reaction). And at no point does anyone indicate that the four-source model of theological reflection is a conversation between the four sources of Tradition, Culture, Experience and Position.

That is one way to introduce – in a manner which is slightly under the radar – the principles and practice of this model of theological reflection to a large group of people. If we were to do this in class, we might do it in a different way. A group of six to eight students are seated around a table on which there are several large flipchart-size pieces of paper and some pens. The group are asked if someone would be willing to offer up a credit or debit card for a few minutes and place it in the middle of the table ('Don't worry – we are not going to cut it up!'). In four distinct places on the paper, the group are asked to write and discuss: (a) what you recall the Scriptures say about money and finance; (b) how the world we live in relates to financial institutions, banks and credit; (c) what your own personal experience of credit or debit cards is; and (e) what do you feel very strongly about with regards finance and credit? The ensuing conversation can run for as long as time permits. The exercise concludes with making sure the card is returned safely to its owner!

In the context of a class introduction, rather than a gentle taster like the induction day above, the conversation would move on quickly to an introduction of the four-source model and an explanation of the sources involved.

It is the conviction of the authors of this book that the four-source model of theological reflection is both nimble and robust. It can be used in an exercise such as the one using a credit card to explore theological aspects of finance in a short space of time; or it can be used over several weeks or months to explore a community or national issue. It can be used to underpin an educational approach, as, for example, in the teaching and forming of people for licensed and ordained ministry; or it can facilitate the lifelong learning of the people of God – a tool to be used for setting God's people free.

Before we explore the model in detail, let us consider the wider context in which the practice of theological reflection locates itself.

Practical theology and theological reflection

The publication of *The Wiley-Blackwell Companion to Practical Theology* (Miller-McLemore, 2012) is an indication that the discipline of practical theology has come of age. Within the wider academy, developments that increasingly place an emphasis on practice, combined with the work of philosophical, political and social theorists, have nudged practical theologians into a reassessment of their own field, resulting in richer conversations between many sub-disciplines. This breadth and variety brings its own conundrum: what is practical theology? Bonnie Miller-McLemore defines it thus:

> Practical theology refers to an activity of believers seeking to sustain a life of reflective faith in the everyday, a method or way of understanding or analysing theology in practice used by religious leaders and by teachers and students across the theological curriculum, a curricular area in theological education focused on ministerial practice and sub-specialties, and, finally, an academic discipline pursued by a smaller subset of scholars to support and sustain these first three enterprises.

She then shows how each understanding points to eight different spatial locations:

> from *daily life* to *library* and *fieldwork* to *classroom, congregation* and *community*, and, finally, to *academic guild* and *global context*. The four understandings are connected and interdependent, not mutually exclusive, however, and reflect the range and complexity of practical theology today.
>
> (Miller-McLemore, 2012, 5)

The glue that holds together the four areas described by Bonnie Miller-McLemore is *theological reflection*, the process whereby believers, religious leaders, teachers, students and scholars make connections between their experience and their faith.

When outlining the rise of practical theology over the last 25 years Elaine Graham describes theological reflection as being 'at its very heart' (Graham, Walton and Ward, 2007, 1), echoing the phrase used by Paul Ballard and John Pritchard that 'theological reflection is at the heart of the nature and task of practical theology' (2006, 127), and Judith Thompson identifies it as the 'defining element' of practical theology (Thompson, Pattison and Thompson, 2008, 18). Stephen Pattison describes it as the 'lodestone and distinguishing mark' (Pattison, Thompson and Green, 2003, 119) and Elizabeth Conde-Frazier, working in the Latina context of north Philadelphia, an area hurt badly by economic decline, stresses that it has to be earthed. In offering a definition she borrows a phrase from Charles Melchert (1998, 94):

> Theological reflection is not detached rationality but relates 'the sores of the body and scars of the soul.'
>
> (Conde-Frazier, 2012, 239)

In a similar vein Mary McClintock Fulkerson's study, rooted in the life of a local congregation, refers to the wounds the community bears, stressing the 'primacy of the situation for theological reflection' (2007, 235). Valburga Schmiedt Streck asserts that in Brazil theological reflection 'cannot be seen as separate from the concept of social exclusion and poverty or from political involvement in the struggle for social and economic justice' (2012, 525). Terry Veling sees practical theology as an attempt to heal the age-old division between systematic and pastoral theology, so that theological reflection regains its 'intrinsic connection to life' (2005, 5).

From 1969 to 1973 David Jenkins was Director of the World Council of Churches Humanum Studies; he was one of the first people to offer a written definition,[1] describing theological reflection as:

> that activity, or all those activities, which seek to bring theology to bear on our life problems so that there is a faithfulness, discernment and judgement.
>
> (1971a, 4)

He is convinced theological reflection is a communal activity involving theologians together with all other specialist resources – this does not really become an established way of looking at theological reflection until much later, which means he was a nascent practical theologian.

In a report to the CCIA[2] Executive Committee he argues persuasively for human rights to be viewed from a theological perspective. He concludes:

> Thus we need continual theological reflection on our programmes and practices with regard to human rights. I would suggest that a central purpose of this theological reflection would be to *disturb us* and to encourage us to disturb much that is taken for granted. For theology is

to do with God and God as seen in the Bible and as seen in Jesus Christ is surely the God who constantly disturbs patterns, policies and powers so that men may be free to seek their fulfilment in one another in Him and in Him in one another.

(1971b, 5)

Theological reflection should disturb us.

When I read Jenkins's words in their original medium, it is a powerful reminder of the context in which this work was being done. The notes are typed and bound – this is the era before the widespread use of computers and instant communication. An era, perhaps, when there was time to reflect before action was demanded.

Looking back over 40 years later, Paul Ballard perceives all five of the models of contextual theology identified by Bevans (1992) present in practical theology and two in particular in theological reflection: the critical-correlational model of systematic theology and the pastoral cycle of liberation theology.

Critical dialogue between the present reality and the tradition lies at the heart of both models. This encounter has increasingly become known as 'theological reflection' and is the heart of the practical theological method.

(Ballard, 2012, 168)

This book will attempt to demonstrate how these two models, both of which have a dialogical element, nourish an overt conversational model from which emerges a more refined and intentional practice of theological reflection.

Frustration with theological reflection

Despite all these accolades for theological reflection there has still existed for some time a frustration among adult educators that even though they themselves grasp the importance of theological reflection the practice still does not appear to be rooted in ministerial practice.

It is now nearly 30 years since Stephen Pattison penned his article 'Some straw for the bricks' (1989).[3] In this ground-defining work he laments that generations of students on pastoral placements within colleges and courses around the country were consistently asked to undertake theological reflection on their experience without being equipped with the appropriate tools to do so; they were being asked to make bricks without straw. Fifteen years later he reports that the situation has still not improved, as he and his co-authors found that newly ordained clergy were scathing about the usefulness of this model, describing their experience as dismal (Pattison, Thompson and Green, 2003, 129). Despite its widespread use there is still a flow of reports that suggest all is not well. Judith Thompson and her colleagues say they found a frustrating lack of clarity among students about what theological reflection is (Thompson, Pattison and Thompson, 2008, viii), and Graeme Smith bemoans that students at his institution simply do not 'get it' (2008, 31).

The predominant model used for theological reflection in the UK, especially among those involved in some form of ministerial formation or training, is the *pastoral cycle*.[4] Rooted in the work of Juan-Luis Segundo's *Liberation of Theology* (1977) and Kolb's learning cycle (1984), its influence is not to be underestimated – Mary Clark Moschella refers to it as the 'famous pastoral cycle' (2012, 229). It was introduced in the UK by Laurie Green in 1990, and supported by Paul Ballard and John Pritchard six years later (1996).

In the last few years Helen Cameron has been involved in five works that champion its use: *Resourcing Mission* (Cameron, 2010); *Talking about God in Practice* (Cameron, Bhatti, Duce, Sweeney and Watkins, 2010); *Theological Reflection for Human Flourishing* (Cameron, Reader, Slater and Rowland, 2012); *Researching Practice in Ministry and Mission* (Cameron and Duce, 2013) and *Just Mission* (Cameron, 2015). The popularity of the pastoral cycle and its apparent simplicity exacerbates the problem of ineffective theological reflection because the model is used uncritically and, with a monopoly in the field, has no other model acting as a critical friend or challenger. We wanted our students to engage in a model that encourages them to dig down more deeply, to creatively disturb in the way Jenkins anticipated, and so we turned to the four-source model, seeking first to understand it more fully and then place it in conversation with the pastoral cycle.

Historical roots and theological provenance

For five years in the late 1970s James and Evelyn Eaton Whitehead were graduate theology faculty and co-directors of the Office of Field Education in Ministry, University of Notre Dame. In 1978 they founded Whitehead Associates as consultants in education and ministry and two years later published *Method in Ministry* (1980). The introduction opens with:

> Theological reflection in ministry is the process of bringing to bear in the practical decisions of ministry the resources of the Christian faith.

They swiftly differentiate between *model* and *method*.

> In this book we propose both a model and a method for doing theo-
> logical reflection in ministry. In the model we indicate three sources
> of information that are relevant to decision making in contemporary
> ministry: the Christian Tradition, personal experience, and cultural
> information. In the method we suggest a three-step process – attending,
> assertion, and decision – through which the information is clarified,
> coordinated, and allowed to shape pastoral action.
>
> (Whitehead and Whitehead, 1980, 1)

This differentiation between model and method is a useful working
definition which we will adopt as we journey through this book.

The Whiteheads openly acknowledge that theological reflection in
ministry is not new (1980, 1), and indicate that there are two sources
from which models of theological reflection have been developed, which
they describe as theology and ministry.

In theology they identify the work of Paul Tillich on systematics (1951)
and culture (1959); Bernard Lonergan (1972) and David Tracy (1975) are
acknowledged on theological method. In ministry they acknowledge the
influences of methods of Clinical Pastoral Education (CPE).[5]

The three sources they depict as:

- Tradition – pluriform in Scripture and history,
- Personal Experience – what the individual believer and the community
  bring to the reflection,
- Cultural information – data from the culture (e.g. social sciences) that
  influence the issue.

> (Whitehead and Whitehead, 1980, 14)

The principal driving force in this model of reflection is a 'ministerial
concern'. Using examples drawn from parish life the authors suggest that

> The model of theological reflection in ministry suggests resources that
> can help persons in ministry to respond faithfully and effectively to the
> concerns that challenge the community of faith.
>
> (Whitehead and Whitehead, 1980, 21)

The process of the model is understood as several overlapping stages
which produce a three-stage method. These are summarized as:

I ATTENDING
Seek out the information on a particular pastoral concern that is available in personal experience, Christian Tradition, and cultural sources.

II ASSERTION
Engage the information from these three sources in a process of mutual clarification and challenge in order to expand and deepen religious insight.

III DECISION
Move from insight through decision to concrete pastoral action.

(Whitehead and Whitehead, 1980, 24)

It is worth noting this book is now nearly 40 years old. James and Evelyn Eaton Whitehead were gently introducing the reader to new approaches to tradition, experience and culture which in the twenty-first century we would not only take for granted but even regard as passé. In examining tradition they survey developments in biblical scholarship, using the work of Raymond Brown (1975; Brown, Murphy and Fitzmyer, 1968) and others to illustrate the pluriform nature of the biblical tradition. In looking at experience they identify a range of theological methods as we identified above but seem to draw back from David Tracy's definition of experience as a common *human* experience and prefer instead a suggestion by Avery Dulles to use *Christian* experience as a source of reflection (1980, 55). In a short chapter on culture there is acknowledgement (though not acceptance?) of the work of liberation theologians though most of the conversation here is with the social sciences. The primary emphasis of the Whiteheads is that these are sources of *information* rather than sources in their own right.

There is no doubt that the model James and Evelyn Eaton Whitehead captured in their 1980 book is a worthy milestone in the 'standing on the shoulders of giants' tradition. What is clearly lacking in the book is any detailed explanation of how an individual or a group moves between the three sources of experience, culture and tradition, and what criteria may be invoked to choose from the many competing voices in all three sources. However, since we recognize it as being one of the works that *began* the process of describing how we do theological reflection, it is not surprising. It is also worth noting that their initial work was done before the publication of Donald Schön's book *The Reflective Practitioner* (1983).

Models and methods

Before we go any further, it is worth revisiting the use of the words model and method.

For the reader or student new to the vast literature on theological reflection there is considerable confusion in practical theology in the use of terms to describe or define theological reflection. Robert Kinast talks about *styles* (2000, 3); Judith Thompson and colleagues use the terms *approaches* and *models* (Thompson, Pattison and Thompson, 2008, 50) and then *variations* on models (2008, 57); Patricia O'Connell Killen and John de Beer refer to nine *processes* (1994, 87). Stephen Pattison appears to use terms synonymously. He talks about a *method* of critical conversation at the beginning of one paragraph and concludes the same paragraph by talking about a *model* of conversation (2000, 139). Elaine Graham and colleagues are very clear that their working term is *method* and use the word in an eminent tradition of theologians who work with *types* (2005, 13). However, a careful reading reveals she swaps between *method*, *model* and *type* (Graham, Walton and Ward, 2005, 12) and in the second volume when recapping the work of the first volume states, 'Theological Reflection Methods set out seven different "models" or exemplary methods of reflection' (Graham, Walton and Ward, 2007, 2).

Richard Osmer even eschews the word *reflection* and instead talks about making sense of our experience by using theological *interpretation* rooted in four different *tasks* (2008, 1–29).

As we saw above, the Whiteheads were quick to differentiate between *model* and *method*. In their language the term *model* is reserved for the basic type or approach of theological reflection and the term *method* for different versions of the type or approach. So, for example, the pastoral cycle is a *model* of theological reflection and Laurie Green (1990) writes about his *method* of the pastoral cycle model.

A disciplined use of the terms as first suggested and used by the White-heads minimizes the possibility of confusion and establishes a standard terminology. The *model* indicates the sources that are to be used. The *method* indicates the steps by which correlation or conversation is established between the sources (1980, 1). The terms are used consistently in this way throughout this book.

An emerging four-source model

The earliest suggestion for a four-source model comes in an article for the journal *Chicago Studies* in 1983, by Patricia O'Connell Killen and John de Beer, '"Everyday" theology: a model for religious and theological education'. They offer a model for organizing what they call the flow of life: four categories of Tradition, Culture, Positions and Action, describing human experience, which they name a 'a four-source model':[6]

> Visualize it as a figure in three dimensions composed of thin glass rods connecting the four sources. Think of the four sources as the intersecting points of the tetrahedron and think of them as connected by rods.

Planning religious education involves focusing one or more of the four sources and deciding how to connect them.

(Killen and de Beer, 1983, 196)

This is not cited anywhere outside the E*f*M community, which means that the general reader relies upon their later work, *The Art of Theological Reflection* (1994), a more accessible source and widely cited by other writers.

In this well-known work they never explicitly refer to their process of theological reflection as a four-source model. This is because, for them, the primary purpose of theological reflection is exploring experience in conversation with the wisdom of a religious heritage (1994, viii). They describe the process as:

1 Focusing on some aspect of *experience*.
2 Describing that experience to identify the *heart of the matter*.
3 Exploring the heart of the matter in conversation with the wisdom of the *Christian heritage*.
4 Identifying from this conversation *new truths and meanings* for living.

(1994, 74)

This *flow* of experience they represent as a prism (see Figure 1).

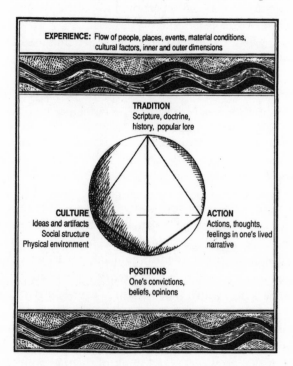

Figure 1 Killen and de Beer's prism of experience (1994, 60)

By contrast, material from E*f*M (in Sewanee, 2003) says:

> Our experience indicates that theological reflection is more likely to occur if we differentiate personal experience and experience of the world and are careful to distinguish among four sources: Personal Experience/Action, Personal Position (Beliefs, Values), Culture/Society, and the Christian Tradition. The Action and Position sources reflect personal experiences and beliefs, while Culture and Tradition identify what we receive from the world.
>
> (Education for Ministry, 2013)

The E*f*M community has consistently referred to the process of reflection they use as the 'four-source model' as can be seen from Ed de Bary's use (2003, xvi footnote).

In other words, Patricia Killen and John de Beer are clear that theological reflection involves exploring experience in conversation with the wisdom of a religious heritage, whereas the E*f*M communities have always talked about a four-source model of theological reflection. What we wish to declare emphatically, in our developed version of the model, is that theological reflection is a *conversation between sources.*

Our version of the four-source model

Killen and de Beer's model assumes that everything is based upon experience and then separates that experience into *experience of* Tradition, Culture, Position and Action where Action is the thoughts and feelings associated with a person's actions.

In our practice we name Experience as a source, so that the four sources are *Tradition, Culture, Experience* and *Position,* and define theological reflection as a *conversation between four sources* (see Figure 2).

The key word is 'conversation'. In human conversation trains of thought and contributions are not always sequential or ordered. Voices can retrace their steps, interrupt one another and even go off at a tangent – and of course people sometimes talk at the same time. New connections are being made constantly. There is a tendency to turn theological reflection into something akin to a step programme – once you have done step 4 you must do step 5. It follows that if theological reflection is indeed a 'conversation' then we must both expect, and indeed encourage, the possibility that each of the four sources may speak or be given voice at different points in the conversation.

We would claim that theological reflection is the learned discipline of drawing *all* the four sources of Tradition, Culture, Experience and

Position into an imaginative conversation. The methods we offer in using the model provide a discipline and framework to organize a discussion into what Stephen Pattison has termed a *critical* conversation (1989).

What does the basic model look like in practice? In order to encourage both the disciplined and creative interaction between the four sources we give preference to methods that make use of an image. The process for generating an image is roughly the same whether one is using the methods of Patricia O'Connell Killen and John de Beer or those in this book. For example, I can relate an incident when I was in the middle of a discussion with a class; out of nowhere one of the adult learners began to give me unsolicited feedback, saying that recently I had said something that for her was helpful. In front of the rest of the group she vividly outlined how affirmed she had been and how wonderful my comments were. Recalling the moment and attending to my feelings, I remember I was embarrassed, flattered and pleased. What was it like? It was like being given a large bouquet of flowers.

In a few short steps I have recalled an experience (teaching), identified the heart of the matter (embarrassment at being praised), and turned the heart of the matter into an image (receiving a bouquet of flowers). I can now use this image to make connections to Tradition, Culture and Position.

In this method the image is at the heart of the reflection. We imagine this image as being at the heart of a tetrahedron of sources (Figure 2).

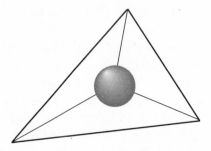

Figure 2 The model

The four sources form one each of the four faces of a tetrahedron, with the image in the epicentre. In order to travel from one source to another it is necessary to travel through the image. This image therefore acts as a bridge or metaphor (carrying meaning) between the four sources.

Our contention (and experience) is that the four-source model is a neglected resource, in part because the way in which it has been developing in new ways in different communities is relatively unknown. This book seeks to give a voice to these communities of practice by sharing their experiences, as they have been drawn together through the co-operative inquiry groups, and offering in detail different methods.

We recognize a significant difference has emerged between the Killen and de Beer model, which sits in the correlational tradition as defined by Paul Ballard – lived experience in conversation with the Christian heritage – and the way we have developed the model, which sees tradition as a source to be drawn on, not an unquestioned authority.

Before we leave this chapter, the dynamic way in which theological reflection has been evolving in different communities may be seen briefly by revisiting the Whiteheads' work. In 1995 they published a second edition of the 1980 book (Whitehead and Whitehead, 1995). In one sense it is the same book because it contains the same argument and has the same shape. However, the content is vastly different. Benefiting from a slimming down of the original version, what is very striking is the change in the use of language. For example:

correlation	*becomes*	conversation
pole	→	partner
the minister	→	faith community
cultural information	→	culture
decision	→	pastoral response
ideal	→	goal
Catholic	→	catholic

There is a real sense that reflection has ceased to be the prerogative of male clergy (which was the original context of much of their work) and become the vocation of the people of God; note too how culture is growing into a genuine source rather than simply a vessel or imparter of information.

From a general consideration of the emergence of the model we now turn to how we have developed and used it in practice. This is elaborated through research that gathers and synthesizes expertise quarried from both the public and private domains combined with new data generated by an original form of action research.

Notes

1 There are earlier passing references to theological reflection in the 1960s, but the phrase tends to be used without offering a definition, which seems to suggest that although the phrase might appear in written form it was not yet used intentionally as a concept. For example, Richard Comstock in an article for the journal *Soundings* in 1968 titled 'Marshall McLuhan's theory of Sensory Form: a theological reflection', despite placing the phrase in his title, uses it only once in the main text: 'McLuhan has reminded us that it would be a mistake if attention to the importance

of time for theological reflection obscures the importance and relevance of space as well (Comstock, 1968).' In the same year James Bergland clearly indicates that the phrase is coming into use in the ministerial training institutions, when looking at the experience of American students in field education (what in this country we call placements), and gives some insight as to why a definition has not yet been concretely formed:

> The concept 'theological reflection' itself became increasingly difficult to define. Since everyone knew what each word meant, it seemed logical that we would all know the meaning of their combination in a phrase. Yet in a vocationally and theologically pluralistic setting with maximum variables in effect, the phrase 'thinking theologically' seemed to become increasingly vague, referring to a many-faceted, high-variable and unstable process which, signifying almost everything, perhaps signified nothing in particular.
>
> (Bergland, 1969, 341)

2 Commission of the Churches on International Affairs.

3 The article is frequently accessed through Woodward, Pattison and Patton's *The Blackwell Reader in Pastoral and Practical Theology*, where it is reprinted in full (1999).

4 See Paul Ballard and John Pritchard (2006, 82–6). They summarize the cycle as a fourfold action: Experience, Exploration, Reflection and Action.

5 There is a strong tradition of CPE in the United States dating as far back as the 1920s and the work of Anton Boisen. Students, traditionally seminarians, are exposed to the realities of pastoral care through fieldwork placements, e.g. hospitals, and are then expected to reflect theologically on this experience.

6 The formatting of the phrase is as used by Killen and de Beer.

2

Researching the model

GARY O'NEILL

The journal *Systemic Practice and Action Research* had a special issue in 2002 dedicated to the practice of co-operative inquiry in which Peter Reason commented:

> I have been struck how much the people who I talk to about co-operative inquiry want to hear *stories*:[1] not just the theory and methodology, but the human stories about how it all works. They want to know how to initiate an inquiry group, how many people to include, how long the inquiry should go on for, how to locate an inquiry within an organization. In particular, they want to know about the personal qualities this kind of inquiry will demand, the attitudes and skills they will be required to manifest.
>
> (2002, 169)

As indicated in the Introduction, this chapter may not be of interest to you if your main concern is how to use the four-source model. However, if you are interested in the practicalities of research, then what follows takes Peter Reason's enthusiasm to heart and gives a glimpse into one researcher's methodology and experience.

A basic grasp of what is outlined in this chapter also helps to understand why frequent references to the work of several theological reflection groups are made in subsequent chapters.

The researcher

I began my process of research by identifying who I am and how this influences both my research and my reflexivity. I describe myself as a reflective practitioner (Schön, 1983). A white British man, born into a working-class family, married with two adult children and 60 years old; I enjoy a middle-class lifestyle. I began training as an adult educator 35 years ago, specializing in group process and the designing of structured experiential learning. I am the Director of Studies for Ordinands in the

Diocese of Chester, one of the foundation partners in the All Saints Centre for Mission and Ministry (All Saints) in the north-west of England,[2] where I lead modules in theological reflection, ministry, and liturgy, teaching those preparing for ordained and licensed ministry.

I am the voluntary Director of EfM in the United Kingdom;[3] I have been a mentor[4] and trainer[5] since 1992, which means that I have considerable experience in *doing* theological reflection as a mentor of a group, as a trainer of mentors, and as a trainer of the trainers of mentors internationally. I am a member of the British and Irish Association for Practical Theology. I stand at an intersection: I work in the academy and am an adult educator in a ministerial college. As an ordained Anglican of over 35 years, I exercise a priestly ministry in my local parish. The overlap of my roles is illustrated in Figure 3.

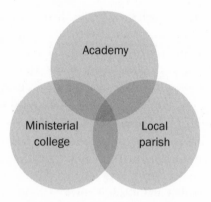

Figure 3 The researcher's context

This personal information is given out of a realization that my context shapes my work and is, I believe, good practice. I concur with Nod Miller when she affirms:

> I recognize that aspects of my life history and of my identity, such as gender, generation, ethnicity, sub-cultural affiliations, and professional location, will impact on the narrative that I produce and the perspective from which I view its subject matter.

> (2000, 76)

My approach is to draw out, rather than teach or even coach. In adult education this is regarded as similar to the contrast Paulo Freire (1972) makes between conscientization and the banking model of learning.

A methodology fit for purpose

What kind of research design is fit for my purpose?

My research interest is theological reflection, and experience informs me that it is best undertaken in a group. I introduce it to my adult learners in a group context and this approach is endorsed by other practical theologians. This practice is influenced by work in continuing education, which over the last 50 years has moved from a discourse dominated by behaviourism to the andragogy of Malcom Knowles (1980) and the social, contextual work of Lev Semyonovich Vygotsky (1962).[6] Confident adult learners, immersed in this collaborative co-learning culture, would not warm to being researched upon, so I looked to action research as a way forward; this is consistent with my values.

My values demand that my research approach must have people at its heart, which means going beyond a simple choice over method and considering instead a methodology – a means rather than an end, giving preference to the way the research is conducted over any potential results. It could be argued that this values-based approach risks ignoring a potential research method which might produce better results; if there is a better approach then it is not one I can entertain because this research is not about results, it is about an approach.

An approach to life is a good way to describe action research. It arose as a challenge to more traditional research which is seen as hierarchical, oppressive and often secretive, where subjects are researched and the data produced is guarded jealously by those who undertake the research. Action research is participatory and concerned as much with improving practice as it is with generating new knowledge and data. It is seen by many of its practitioners not simply as a methodology but also as an *orientation to inquiry*. There are a wide number of different types, which is why the approach taken by Peter Reason and Hilary Bradbury in describing action research as a *family of practices* is helpful (2008, 1). This breadth of approach and practice leads them to declare that there can never be any right way of doing action research; rather than attempt a precise definition, they prefer to offer a description.

A first description of action research is that it

- is a set of practices that responds to people's desire to act creatively in the face of practical and often pressing issues in their lives in organizations and communities;
- calls for engagement *with* people in collaborative relationships opening new 'communicative spaces'[7] in which dialogue and development can flourish;
- draws on many ways of knowing, both in the evidence that is generated

in inquiry and in its expression in diverse forms of presentation as we share learning with wider audiences;

- is values oriented, seeking to address issues of significance concerning the flourishing of human persons, their communities, and the wider ecology in which we participate;
- is a living, emergent process that cannot be predetermined but changes and develops as those engaged deepen their understanding of the issues to be addressed and develop their capacity as co-inquirers both individually and collectively.

(2008, 3)

Action research encourages the values of the research to be openly named and utilized. It is congruent with my values since it is a way of researching *with* people, treating learners as adults who have responsibility for this learning. This is consistent with changing discourse in adult education as exemplified by Daniel D. Pratt and Tom Nesbit, who assert that effective learning is social, contextual, and precipitates questions about power, particularities of circumstances and settings (2000, 122). The only way to ensure this is to hand as much control and influence to the learners as possible.

Cooperative inquiry

Within the field of action research, I chose the research method of co-operative inquiry which I was first introduced to while studying for my MA in 2004. As part of that (MA) dissertation I attempted to form a co-operative inquiry group, but those invited were unable to do so at the time and the research was subsequently undertaken using a different methodology. This highlights a characteristic of a co-operative inquiry group, which is, that since the research is undertaken *with* people, a lone facilitator or researcher cannot make a co-operative inquiry group – by definition it requires co-operation. What I learned from this experience is that an interest in the area of research is not sufficient to encourage commitment to a group – what is needed is a more obvious benefit in the outcome of the research for the individual.

John Heron defines co-operative inquiry as follows:

Co-operative enquiry involves two or more people researching a topic through their own experience of it, using a series of cycles[8] in which they move between this experience and reflecting together on it. Each person is co-subject in the experience phases and co-researcher in the reflection phases.

(1996, 1)

The very nature of co-operative inquiry taps into both my skills and my values. It has integrity with my values for collaboration, inclusion and working experientially. In particular, this means the ability to work in the present – to be able, on the one hand, to offer appropriate facilitation and leadership as a co-member of the group and, on the other, to be reflexive in the opportunity granted by the feedback offered by one's peers in an experiential group.

John Heron describes an experiential[9] group as one in which:

> learning takes place through an active and aware involvement of the whole person – as a spiritually, energetically and physically endowed being encompassing feeling and emotion, intuition and imaging, reflection and discrimination, intention and action.
>
> (1999, 1)

As a feminist I believe that co-operative inquiry, of all the possible action research methods available, is par excellence feminist. However, I note that only two of the projects in the collection of qualitative research projects *The faith lives of women and girls* (Slee, Porter and Phillips, 2013) use an overtly action research approach; Emma Rothwell describes 'Broken silence' as a small-scale piece of feminist action research (2013, 131) and Susanna Gunner in 'Integrating ritual' takes great care to ensure the research methodology is grounded in right relationships (2013, 141). She is inspired by Nicola Slee who, in tracing the development of feminist research methodology, notes the contribution to experiential research undertaken by Shulamit Reinharz.

> Feminists widely advocated a 'participatory model' (Reinharz, 1983) which would aim at producing non-hierarchical, non-manipulative research relationships with the potential to overcome the separation between researcher and researched, and to allow the subjectivity of both to be placed centre stage in the research enterprise.
>
> (2004, 44)

In choosing co-operative inquiry as part of my research methodology I am positioning myself as someone who desires to place people at the heart of *our* research. I paid attention in the co-operative inquiry groups to issues of power, authority and influence in order to attempt to remain faithful to genuine collaboration; one of the crucial ways in which this is made manifest is the decision each group takes with regard to the use of the data.

I draw upon John Heron's work (1996) as a handbook and resource both for myself and the members of the co-operative inquiry groups as together we develop the skills necessary for co-operative inquiry. In my role as the initiator and facilitator I am guided in particular by John Heron's work on facilitation (1989, 1999).

Role of the researcher

The nature of my role is a key question in the inquiry, given that the participants in each group are all members of E*f*M with different roles within that community. Kathryn Herr and Gary Anderson refer to a person's role in research as *positionality* (2005, 29–48). They offer a continuum for the researcher with six defined roles (2005, 31). Ruard Ganzevoort uses images from sport to illustrate four roles of the researcher (2009, 10). I have mapped them against Herr and Anderson (Table 1a).

Herr and Anderson	Ganzevoort	Person order
1. Insider	Player	**First-person**
2. Insider in collaboration with others		
3. Insider(s) in collaboration with outsider(s)	Coach	**Second-person**
4. Reciprocal collaboration (insider-outsider teams)	Referee	
5. Outsider(s) in collaboration with insider(s)	Commentator	**Third-person**
6. Outsider(s) studies insider(s)		

Table 1a Researcher roles

I have developed the Ganzevoort model to make more use of the continuum and utilizes an idea generated by a comment from Jonathan Agnew that the difference between cricket and football commentators is that the former still fly on the same aircraft, share the same hotel and drink in the same bar as the players, whereas football commentators (you may infer from his article) are cosseted superstars who have distanced themselves from the players (2010).[10] While acknowledging the risk of pushing the sporting image too far, since all these roles describe an individual's relationship to a team (whether within or without), an optional role is captain. In groups the role of mentor or facilitator of each stage of the research was undertaken by different members of the group, not by me as the researcher. In my redefined list of roles, a captain could be a player with a specific responsibility; in a co-operative inquiry group a captain is a facilitator or mentor (Table 1b).

Based on my experience of the pilot group, I anticipated that my role in the planned co-operative inquiry groups would oscillate between the roles of player and player-coach. I would seek to be a player to uphold the primary principle of a co-operative inquiry group, that all participation and decision-making is done co-operatively. However, there are two scenarios where it would be necessary for me to be a player-coach: establishing the content of the inquiry and the method of research. In John Heron's terms, this is contracting (1996, 39) and initiating (1996, 62).

Heron identifies three different ways in which a co-operative inquiry group may be launched (1996, 38–9). One or two initiating researchers put out a call to invite others who may have similar interest in joining a co-operative inquiry group – he calls this approach *the initiator's call*. A second possibility might be that an existing group, which has a research topic in mind and has heard about co-operative inquiry, requires assistance with their research; he names this *a call for initiators*. The third way he calls the *boot-strap group*. This is a group of people who decide together that they wish to undertake some research, and having heard about co-operative inquiry, decide to use the approach and in the process train themselves in the methodology. He regards his book *Co-operative Inquiry* as being a manual for members of a boot-strap group. The co-operative inquiry groups I initiated fell into the first and third of his descriptions; I made the call by inviting people to join a co-operative inquiry group, while recognizing that my skills in this area were still limited, so there is a real sense in which each group was also a boot-strap co-operative inquiry group.

Herr and Anderson	Ganzevoort	Ganzevoort developed	Person order
1. Insider		Player	
2. Insider in collaboration with others	Player	Player coach	**First-person**
3. Insider(s) in collaboration with outsider(s)	Coach	Coach	**Second-person**
4. Reciprocal collaboration (insider-outsider teams)	Referee	Referee	
5. Outsider(s) in collaboration with insider(s)	Commentator	Cricket commentator	**Third-person**
6. Outsider(s) studies insider(s)		Football commentator	

Table 1b Researcher roles

My developed Ganzevoort model positions me in relation to the groups.

David Coghlan and Teresa Brannick use four quadrants to describe the relationship of the research and researcher to the institution (Figure 4). In this analysis I would find myself in quadrant 3 with an aspiration that the outcome of the research might lead to a consideration of quadrant 4. My context is more complex in that I am relating to more than one organization.

RESEARCHER

**No Intended Self-Study
in Action**

	1. Traditional research approaches: collection of survey data ethnography case study	2. OD action research: internal consulting
SYSTEM No Intended Self-Study in Action		Intended Self-Study in Action
	3. Individual engaged in reflective study of professional practice	4. Large-scale transformational change Learning history

**Intended Self-Study
in Action**

Figure 4 Researcher and institution: Coghlan and Brannick (2014, 123)

The driving force for my research stems from my work with students and colleagues in All Saints, but I chose to undertake my research in the Education for Ministry programme because the opportunities in Exploring faith Matters are limited by number and All Saints by inexperience. I am therefore a researcher whose paid and majority work is in All Saints, a voluntary director of a small charity, Exploring faith Matters, in quadrant 3 connected within Education for Ministry. There is of course an empathy from all three institutions connected by a concern for theological reflection, so it is not like working in a foreign country, rather more akin to having reading rights in one university based upon membership of another (See Figure 5).

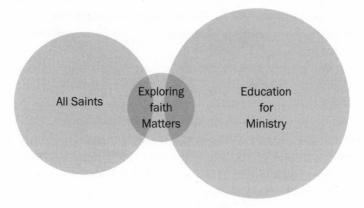

Figure 5 Institutional relationships

Initiating the inquiry groups

A fundamental question was: Who should I invite? My experience of recruiting for the MA suggested that a strong personal interest in theological reflection was required. The only people who regularly participated in theological reflection groups using the four-source model in the UK were EfM groups. However, that network is relatively small,[11] with only a couple of trainers and a handful of mentors on whom I had already drawn for the pilot group. I needed to use the international dimension of the EfM community. This would bring both cultural diversity and a much wider field of experienced practitioners to draw from, and since those invited had all completed the EfM program[12] they would enjoy a solid theological education.[13]

With the concepts of insider and outsider inquiry in mind, combined with my knowledge of the EfM network internationally, I decided that the best way to initiate my co-operative inquiry groups would be to send out an invitation using the existing structures of E*f*M. My first port of call was to contact the directors of E*f*M in each of the four countries in which I wanted to form co-operative inquiry groups. The response of each of these directors and their organizations was different and each of these contributed to the context in which the research took place.[14] This led to the establishing of co-operative inquiry groups in New Zealand, Australia (two groups), the USA and Canada.[15]

As an action researcher within my own organization there is integrity, honesty and sensitivity to the recognition that my view of reality will be different from that of others. As Kathryn Herr and Gary Anderson observe, research takes place in a political world (2005, 64–8). How my research might change the practice of theological reflection is an issue for my wider work; however, how the practice of the organization affects the research method is important here. Stephen Kemmis argues,

> Transforming practices therefore requires not only changing the knowledge (or habitus) of practitioners and others who participate in a practice, but also changing these fields (and other extra-individual features of practice). Changing extra-individual features of practice can be difficult because cultures and discourses, social connections and solidarities, and material-economic arrangements exist between and beyond the individuals whose particular actions enact, but do not by themselves constitute, practices.
>
> (2008, 126)

Although all six groups contributed generously to my research and five international Directors of E*f*M were involved (including this researcher), my experience and observation is that none was without a political dimension. The two most vibrant groups were in Australia, where four days were devoted exclusively to each co-operative inquiry group, the number of participants was high, the invitation to participate was strong and the director highly motivated; participants gained accreditation for participation.[16] Auckland was a good-sized group but it was contained within the constraints of a network event which was dealing with some of its own historical process and in the context of a country living with the aftermath of earthquakes. The Sewanee[17] and Kelowna groups were small. The processes at work are complex but the simple observation is that the major player, the home of the programme and best resourced, formed the smallest group.

The research cycles

There were six inquiry groups that met in the following order: Oxford, UK (pilot); Auckland, New Zealand; Brisbane and Melbourne, Australia; Sewanee, USA; and Kelowna, Canada. The events ranged in length from two to four days, had a mix of trainers and mentors, and ranged in group size from four to twelve members. The 47 co-researchers completed 34 cycles[18] of inquiry generating 79 possible research questions (see Figure 6).[19] These statistics are provided to give the reader an overall *impression* of the landscape of the co-operative inquiry groups' work and are not offered as quantitative data. They help to appreciate the geographical spread of the groups, relative size and the sheer volume of possible research questions the research cycles generated; the detailed data from the groups is therefore only a fraction of that available. I had wondered at the planning stage if six groups were sufficient and was therefore genuinely surprised both at the amount of data produced and the energy carried from one to the next.

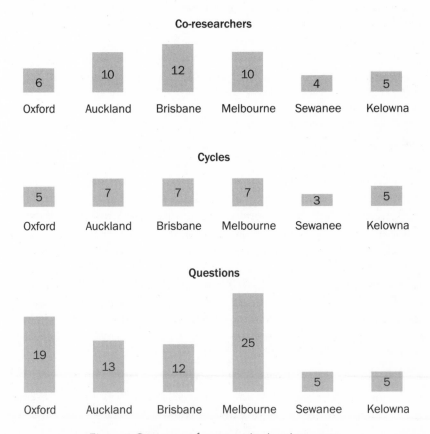

Co-researchers

Oxford	Auckland	Brisbane	Melbourne	Sewanee	Kelowna
6	10	12	10	4	5

Cycles

Oxford	Auckland	Brisbane	Melbourne	Sewanee	Kelowna
5	7	7	7	3	5

Questions

Oxford	Auckland	Brisbane	Melbourne	Sewanee	Kelowna
19	13	12	25	5	5

Figure 6 Summary of co-operative inquiry groups

Still at the panoramic level, Figure 7 shows that two-thirds of the research cycles' areas were common to two groups and very nearly as many to at least three groups. The distribution suggests that the work of the pilot group may have primed the pump of the initial work of the subsequent five groups.

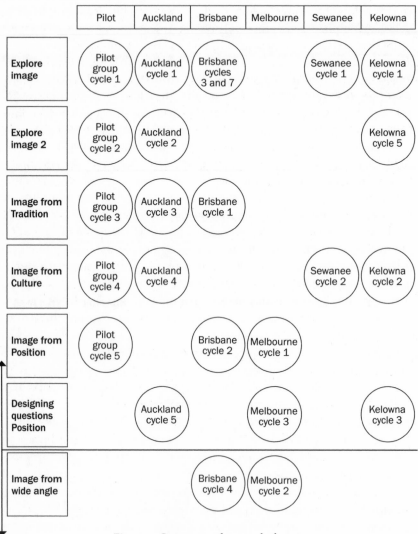

Figure 7 Summary of research themes

In each of the agreed accounts the participants list what they consider to be the learning generated by each cycle (as well as further research questions). My task on reading and re-reading the agreed accounts was to sort the insights generated by the groups into areas or themes. This was an evolving process rather than something that happened once and is similar to that described by John Swinton and Harriet Mowat in the Jacobsfield Vineyard research (2006, 146). My sorting produced six themes:[20] (i) Images; (ii) Interrogatory questions; (iii) The four-source model; (iv) Co-operative inquiry; (v) Learning community; and (vi) The researcher.

Reporting

I noted at the outset of this chapter Peter Reason's encouragement to tell stories about action research. Conversely, John Heron is opposed to the idea that the proper outcome of research with people is a written report (1999, 101). This is rooted in his conviction that the proper outcome is the transformation of people. However, he does concede that reports might have a secondary status as a means of communicating something about co-operative inquiry and the focus of a group's research. He advocates that the report be something everyone contributes to and must be agreed by everyone – in practice, the writing may be done by two or three people or even a single author as long as it is fully owned by the group.

In my research I have not found any precedents in the field of practical theology for examining how the data from a co-operative inquiry group is analysed. Much of action research in practical theology assumes a qualitative approach (Swinton and Mowat, 2006). The extensive field of action research (Reason and Bradbury, 2008) is similarly sparse and educational practice (Koshy, 2010), with obvious parallels to my own teaching, is still silent. The paucity of examples of handling co-operative inquiry group data may be due to the experiential nature of the co-operative inquiry groups. John Heron and Peter Reason, in tracing their own work over four decades, consistently affirm the co-operative nature of the process:

> Co-operative inquiry is a form of second-person[21] action research in which all participants work together in an inquiry group as co-researchers and as co-subjects. *Everyone* is engaged in the design and management of the inquiry; *everyone* gets into the experience and action that is being explored; *everyone* is involved in making sense and drawing conclusions; thus *everyone* involved can take initiative and exert influence on the process. This is not research on people or about people, but research *with* people.
>
> (2008, 366)

My research is primarily *in* the group. However, when talking about this type of inquiry Heron and Reason often assume, or refer to, inquiry groups where part of the research takes place *outside* the group. For example:

> The action phases often involve co-inquirers being busy with their individual action inquiries in everyday life, apart from each other.
>
> (2008, 370)

What is frequently envisaged is a group of practitioners who come together to reflect on their individual practice by sharing and exploring with their peers, and then go back to their relevant field to gain more experience before returning again to the inquiry group. In Cathy Aymer's (2001) account from the field of health and social care, black professionals working in white organizations come together in three inquiry groups to share their experience back in the workplace; Lyle Yorks et al. (2008) and colleagues initiate six co-operative inquiry groups of social justice leaders who meet over a three-year period and between meetings participants both experiment and seek new experiences with which to return to the group; in Kate McArdle's account (2008, 608) of working in a supervisory role to mentor a new facilitator, the extent to which a good deal of work happens outside the group is underlined by her story of friction caused in the group by one person complaining about the lack of work done by others in the group in between cycles; and even in John Heron and Gregg Lahood's charismatic inquiry group, which has a very strong emphasis on the corporate experience of the fortnightly meetings, there is still space given in the session for people to report on spiritual activity undertaken in everyday life, again outside the group (2008, 442). The experiential nature of the co-operative inquiry groups for this research requires that the primary focus is always about what is happening to the group in the present moment. This is the heart of Peter Reason and Hilary Bradbury's principle: 'action research / practice addresses our ability to inquire face-to-face with others into issues of mutual concern' (2008, 6).

In describing co-operative inquiry above I quoted at length John Heron's definition of 'experiential' – paying attention to the whole person and to what is happening in the moment. Any detailed account of such a group would be extremely difficult to produce. At one level there might be a desire for accuracy which would suggest the production of a script of each meeting or video recording because much communication is non-verbal. Agreement on a detailed commentary could either take a long time or be deemed impossible.

However, practitioners in experiential learning often have a clear understanding that they have learned something; this may be intuitive, rational or kinaesthetic (and any combination of the three). John Heron and Peter Reason call this *experiential knowing* (2008, 367) that is based in the *experiential presence* of persons in the world. This type of learning or knowing is difficult to forget or even unlearn because it is a holistic knowing that involves the whole person. In presenting or analysing data it is sometimes difficult to provide written or presentational evidence but the learning is nonetheless long-lasting (Heron and Reason, 2008, 370).

With these considerations in mind the co-operative inquiry groups have not sought to produce a minute-by-minute script of their experience, but a summary of what they sense they experienced and learned. It is natural for these groups to map on flipchart paper what they are doing as they go along, both to make the process open to each person in the group as it evolves, and to provide a record for themselves for when they come to critically review their experience of each session or cycle. The simplest way to record these sheets was to photograph them. The sheets of paper contained each group's 'data' in that whatever the group had learned in a cycle of research was recorded; their data also provided a tool for the groups to use when reviewing and evaluating their learning.

By the end of the second co-operative inquiry group, in Auckland, a convention had been established to differentiate between *raw* and *polished* data. The raw data, assembled quickly, consisted of rough summary notes of each session written by me, combined with photographs of the flip-charts. This was available to group members before the event ended. In this raw account individual names were often included to assist every-one in recalling accurately who did or said what at any one time. In the polished data, produced after the event, the names are removed, and the description simply says, 'a group member' or 'the mentor'. The polished data is the final account of the co-operative inquiry groups and stands as an agreed written record of what they have experienced and learned. These accounts cannot be modified or changed.

The co-operative inquiry accounts uphold both the principle and prac-tice of what John Heron is aiming for. They point to individual and group learning which the validity criteria suggest is long term. Although the accounts do not follow John Heron's 23 bullet points I can see that they have all been addressed (1996, 102–3).

Despite starting with what might be termed a traditional view of research (the groups were my data, to be analysed and used)[22] my own experience convinced me that their story was central. Therefore, to stand by all my co-researchers, I name them in our preface and access to the agreed accounts, which I now hold in trust, is available via the web links in the book's Bibliography.

Refining of research question

I have described how my values and concerns, through a process of reflection, led to my area of research. The distillation into one succinct question was not something that happened early in the process because of the very iterative and generative nature of action research and in particular co-operative inquiry. Part of the commitment to a co-operative inquiry process is the openness to a change of direction or modification of the research question.

From agreed account to annotated story

I regard significant or *experiential learning* as similar to Gillie Bolton's 'aha moment' (2010, xviii) and am conscious that an important aspect of reflective practice is the use of journaling. Experiential learning for me is like learning to swim or ride a bike. There is a 'light bulb moment' at which everything comes together: you *can* swim or ride. When you return from the pool or the bike ride it is not necessary to journal this activity to embed the learning or reflect further upon it. When you return to the pool or ride, your *whole body*,[23] mind and muscles will know how to swim or ride – you will never forget.

The agreed accounts provide a window into the life of the co-operative inquiry groups which, together with my own experientially rooted memory, provide for me a *thick* description of what occurred. The value of this thick approach is the way in which for me it accurately describes what occurred and echoes Joseph Ponterotto's definition, in assigning purpose and intentionality (2006, 543). There is a transition here, from data that I experienced as a member of all the co-operative inquiry groups to the written accounts they generated, and then my critical reflection on both.

I produced a working document for myself that contained the agreed text, alongside which I placed a commentary of my insights and reflections – unlike the agreed accounts, this document is not in the public domain. This researcher account has strong elements of the reflective practice style advocated by Gillie Bolton (2010, xxi) in that my writing and comments reveal as much about myself as they do about what I think is happening at any one particular moment in a group. At the same time it has elements of both a research-driven and writer-driven draft as described by Lucretia Yaghjian (2006, 125–6). This *annotated story* becomes for me the equivalent of a journal, a private space where learning takes place over time. There is a risk here, as with all journals, in that it relies heavily on my reflexive analysis of what is important and furthermore the agreed account on which it relies can neither answer back or be changed.

However, the quality of work done in this private space is to be seen in the catalytic way in which my practice changes – a verifiable outcome.

Analysis, best practice and reflexivity

I am affirmed in my approach by the work of Terry Veling, who describes his own habit of writing in the margins of books akin to the Talmudic scholars' habit. I had not come across this practice so insightfully articulated before and I realized that it is a habit I appropriated long ago. What gives life and power to these jottings in the margin is the realization, as he identifies, that 'the margins represent the vital space between text and reader' (2005, 67).

As the book is turned around by 90 degrees, the margins become literally the physical space between the text and the reader. This is how I would describe my annotated story. It works in the same way as a journal but with a much more immediate and powerful tool as a catalyst to critical reflection on my experience of my research journey both as it unfolds and retrospectively. The reader is, of course, the author of the notes in the margins and the re-reading adds another layer of both experience and insight to the research. In Gillie Bolton's terminology the writing in the margins of co-operative inquiry groups' accounts is *reflection*. And this produces for me my annotated story. Re-reading the annotated story with my reflection notes at the centre is *reflexive*. The annotated story (my 'journal') is the key tool for my *reflective practice* (Bolton, 2010).

Looping back

I noted above, under the section on reporting, a desire to include my co-researchers in the outcome of the research groups. Although space and time prevent the inclusion of comments with whole group approval, it is possible to invite people back into the research via a simple looping-back process. William Torbert and Steven Taylor see *development action inquiry* as a means of testing one's data, interpretations and assumptions (2008, 240). I invited every person who had been a member of a co-operative inquiry group to comment or respond to drafts of my writing. This meant that not only could they read my reflections and the comments of their own group, but also the polished accounts and my comments on all the co-operative inquiry groups. The result of this looping back was encouraging in several ways. First of all, there was no disagreement with anything that I had written about the groups. Second, several replies commented on how the draft drew them back into the experience of their group, confirming that the account contained a thick description of what took place not only for me but also for other co-researchers.

> Thick description leads to thick interpretation, which in turn leads to thick meaning of the research findings for the researchers and participants themselves, and for the report's intended readership.
>
> (Ponterotto, 2006, 543)

A second loop involved the use of several critical friends. Richard Winter and Carol Munn-Giddings identify the difficulty of introducing a critical friend into a group of participants who are working effectively, recognizing that it could easily disturb the process of the group (2001). In a co-operative inquiry group the presence of a critical friend (who by definition has a critical distance and therefore is not a stakeholder) would run the risk of the whole group no longer considering itself to be a co-operative inquiry group. The comments from my critical friends were incorporated into later drafts of my writing.

Notes

1 Peter Reason's italics.

2 Roger Walton (Walton, 2002, 203) writes that even the physical location has an effect on learning.

3 EfM, or Education for Ministry, is a long-distance learning programme established by the University of the South, Sewanee, Tennessee, USA. In the UK it goes under the title 'Exploring faith Matters'.

4 EfM groups consist of 6–12 students with a mentor whose task is to facilitate learning rather than teach. Each mentor is accredited by the programme and undertakes regular training.

5 An EfM trainer trains the mentors identified in the above note. Trainers meet regularly to maintain and develop their skills usually at events called 'training of trainers'.

6 For a more recent discussion on the context of adult learning, see Rosemary Caffarella and Sharan Merriam (2000).

7 My note: Stephen Kemmis has argued that action research emphasizes its *social* nature (2008, 122), and in his proposed definition of critical participatory action research defines communicative space as 'space for collective reflection and self-reflection' (2008, 135).

8 In this book these cycles are referred to as *research cycles* in the work of the co-operative inquiry groups.

9 There are many other ways of defining experiential. See, for example, the eleven definitions in Jennifer Moon's selection from the field of education (2004, 108–9).

10 This prescient comment was reinforced by the subsequent sacking of two Sky commentators in January 2011 (Gibson, 2011).

11 The number of students and groups in the UK peaked at about 150 around

2007 and then went into a slow decline which was not turned around until the end of 2012 when there were 75 students. The situation in the rest of the world was and is quite different. At the time the co-operative inquiry groups were being formed, numbers received from the Director of EfM in Sewanee (personal communication, 26 February 2013) revealed that over 80,000 people had been members of an EfM worldwide group with the USA enrolment peaking at over 8,000 in 2006. In 2013 there were around 7,000 students enrolled in the USA and over 37,000 people had completed the full four years. Canada and Australia had about 350 students, and New Zealand has about half that number. EfM in the Bahamas was about the same size as in the UK. In 2018 US numbers are still strong.

12 The term 'program' and its spelling is the way EfM refers to itself in the American context.

13 The first year centres on the Hebrew Scriptures (Old Testament); the second year offers a study of the New Testament; year three provides study of Christian (Church) history and theology; and ethics constitute study in the fourth year. This grounding in theology is an essential source of straw for the group's theological brick-making.

14 The formation of the co-operative inquiry groups was constrained in part by cost. I relied heavily on the hospitality of the different countries and had to be prepared to work with what they generously offered. Looking back, in the end the groups, as described, did provide sufficient opportunity to gather the data that was needed for the research.

15 More information about the groups is provided under 'research cycles'.

16 See note 14.

17 An unexpected benefit was an invitation to participate in a US training event which resulted in a valuable piece of work on multiple images.

18 A cycle includes the planning, implementation, evaluation and review of an area of research.

19 Each group is self-determining and decides for itself which specific research questions to pursue.

20 The identification of these themes is the equivalent of Morten Levin 'singling out major incidents' (2008, 679).

21 One convention in action research is to locate research in one of three areas as originally defined by William Torbert (1998, 225): first-person, second-person or third-person research.

22 I am sure the reader can infer how this approach flies in the face of action research principles.

23 Learning occurs through the active and aware involvement of the whole person (Heron, 1999, 1).

3

Using the basic model in practice

GARY O'NEILL

As indicated in the Introduction, the model presented in detail in this chapter is the result of co-operative research within the international Education for Ministry programme, the learning community of All Saints Centre for Mission and Ministry, combined with the personal experience and research of the contributors to this book including practising theological reflection in the Exploring faith Matters community. This approach is not intended to be definitive or reified but rather offered as a contribution to the practice of theological reflection; it is offered in a similar spirit to that of Patricia Killen and John de Beer when they encourage practitioners to create their own designs for theological reflection because the design is not what is important, rather that the design or facilitator of the reflection is the 'midwife of the movement towards insight' (1994, 141). The chapter is written in the first person as it draws on my personal research as outlined in the Introduction above.

To make the model both easier to comprehend and handle, the synthesis offered here is arranged to present a clearer picture of both model and methods. This is achieved by identifying the key steps to go from any one of four sources to arrive at an image, and then emphasizing the similarity in approach once the reflection reaches the conversation stage. The generation of an image comprises steps 1–7; the conversation takes place in steps 8–16.

The model and methods are also presented in tabular form, with an accompanying process for recording and mapping a theological reflection, which again highlights the model – see the Glossary.

Working in a group

The use of this model of theological reflection is most effective when undertaken with a group of people. This does not mean that the model cannot be used by an individual working alone, but that the experience and insights generated using the model are greatly enhanced when undertaken by a group of people. The more diverse the experience and background of the group members, the greater the range of insights and theological positions that will be added to the theological reflection conversation.

Working in a group is something that is encouraged by a wide range of practitioners: see for example Judith Thompson (Thompson, Pattison and Thompson, 2008, 145–8); Robert Kinast (2000, 11); Laurie Green (2009, 50); and Paul Ballard and John Pritchard, who conclude that it is 'characteristically a corporate activity' (2006, 144). While Patricia O'Connell Killen and John de Beer assert that theological reflection is best learned and practised in a group (1994, 77), the presentation and style of writing used in the often quoted *The Art of Theological Reflection* is almost entirely in the first person.

A group proposing to undertake a theological reflection greatly benefits from a facilitator. This does not necessarily have to be the leader or some-one in a leadership position in the group; rather, it should be an individual or pair whom the group entrusts to guide them through the theological reflection. They should be familiar with the model of theological reflection and comfortable working with the variety of processes generated by a group of people working together; that is, they should have some under-standing of, and skill in, the facilitation of small groups. This means that they should be open to the processes at work both in the group and in themselves. John Heron refers to this as *emotional competence* or emo-tional intelligence (1996, 124–5 and 169–71). This description of practice assumes the use of a facilitator or pair of facilitators.

Ground rules

A theological reflection group is not a co-operative enquiry group per se (see Chapter 1), but it can exhibit the hallmarks of good practice associated with co-operative inquiry, such as:

- a duty of care to each member of the group
- respect for each individual person in the group
- a respect for culture
- an affirmation of individual dignity, and
- protection from harm.

Richard Winter and Carol Munn-Giddings refer to these as 'ground rules' (2001, 220). Care should be taken to distinguish between ground rules and group norms. Ground rules are provisional rules that a new group agrees to at the beginning of its life, whereas in the field of group process and group dynamics norms emerge during the life of the group – they are sometimes subconscious and provide important data for a skilful facilitator.

The kind of reflection undertaken by the group, *theological* reflection, and the identification of one of the model's sources, namely *position*, suggest two further rules. Theological reflection is an exploration of the divine and one of the ways in which this is accomplished is by worship. It is therefore good practice for a theological reflection group either to incorporate prayer into their work or to ensure that it is rooted in the worship of the wider community. My experience of the use of prayer in theological reflection stems from two very contrasting experiences. In the co-operative inquiry groups, corporate prayer was important in maintaining the life of the groups. On the other hand, in my work with students who are inexperienced and, in some cases, still developing emotional competence, the use of prayer can be insensitive, inappropriate or manipulative. This is usually due to an individual's lack of awareness of the effect of their actions on those around them. While the positive use of prayer is often commented on (Thompson, Pattison and Ross, 2008, 245) its misuse is not.

In my experience there are several risks with prayer in a newly formed group. The first is that unless the context is very formal – that is, there is an extremely strong expectation that prayer will take place in a specific way (because that is what always happens here) – it is likely the task of leading prayer will fall to one individual, who will probably extemporize. Since the group is new, how does she know what are the expectations or spiritual practices of the rest of the group? What might then follow is a time of prayer or worship that makes one or more members of the group uncomfortable because it is not sensitive to their way of praying. Two extreme examples might be on the one hand asking people to pray out loud for each other in pairs or, on the other, praying a traditional prayer followed by Hail Mary!

The second might be that the prayers are simply inappropriate because the person tasked does not have the necessary skill or insight to lead them and they are overly personal, parochial or position oriented. The worse outcome is that they are manipulative; the person leading the prayers uses them as an opportunity to set their own agenda or steer the group into a particular course of action under the pretext of seeking God's will. Perhaps the only safe way to pray at the beginning of the life of a group is through a short silence, and even that might make someone uncomfortable. All of which is why building community is important.

Building community

Establishing ground rules contributes to the building of a learning community which the research shows is crucial to the effectiveness of a theological reflection group. Sometimes a group moves quite slowly and at other times breathtaking speed. The process is ongoing, but some thought can be given, by the facilitator or the group at the beginning of its life, about how the process may be encouraged. If the group engages in worship and takes time to set ground rules, then the process will already have begun. How much more time – over and above setting ground rules – can be given to building community depends entirely on the time resources of the group. A proven way of doing this is to share faith stories in which individuals share something of the way in which they have perceived God at work in their lives.

In EfM these are called spiritual autobiographies. The divine aspect is often missed by many storytellers either because it is too sensitive, or the purpose of the exercise is not fully understood. In looking at language, the Kelowna group suggested the phrase 'faith stories' rather than spiritual autobiography; this makes the activity feel less like an exercise and steers people away from simply being autobiographical – where they were born, grew up and so on.

The extent to which the group intentionally spends time at the beginning of a group building community is an important consideration for the facilitator.

Beginning the reflection

The reflection can begin in any one of the four sources. Since the model is essentially a conversation *between* four sources, or four voices (Experience, Tradition, Culture and Position), this insight may seem self-evident. However, research and experience show that those new to this model of theological reflection find it difficult to comprehend this simple idea; there is often initial scepticism that the reflection can begin from certain sources, particularly position or culture. This scepticism is strengthened when it is suggested that the reflection beginning from any of the sources will produce an image to be explored. Within the EfM community, the culture of different groups is likely to result in a group norm for reflection from one source. Outside the EfM community, the four-source model is most likely to be used starting with the experience source, because many students in ministerial colleges and courses will be seeking to use the model to reflect on ministerial practice. My research noted that each of the co-operative inquiry groups, at some point in their work, tested the principle that the four sources are all valid places to start.

Mapping the reflection

The way in which a reflection is laid out or recorded can have a significant impact on the quality of the reflection; it enables each participant to track the progress of the reflection and continually holds before the group the *whole* reflection. An exemplar is offered in Figure 8. Recording the reflection is not prescriptive; there is no 'right' way. However, the example illustrates two principles. First, the four sources are central in helping participants to see the model and, second, subsidiary work that is important, though not central (for example, the thought showering of tradition), is kept to one side of the main workspace. This keeps the mapping clean and the focus clear.

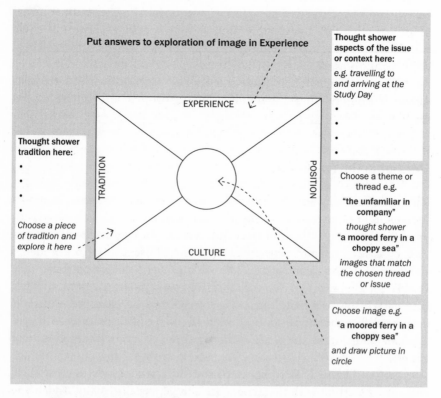

Figure 8 Mapping a theological reflection from a shared experience

The use of an image

In this book we often talk about the use of an image. This is the term used by Killen and de Beer whereas EfM materials emanating from Sewanee frequently use the term 'metaphor' to describe the picture or image that arises in a theological reflection. The word 'metaphor', though technically a useful term to describe how meaning can be carried over from one part of reflection to another,[1] does evoke other meanings that can lead to confusion, especially when people have different and varied understandings of English grammar. In the four-source model, an image is a way of describing the essence of something, the *heart of the matter*.

It is worth spending a few moments to explore your own use of pictures and images. In a Western culture that has moved rapidly to ever shorter versions of the written word (from letter to email to texting to Twitter) the sound bite is increasingly sought after and one of the ways to craft it is to use an image. Politicians have always used them. A government minister in the UK used his resignation press conference to describe working with his former boss as 'walking through mud' (Watt, 2014). Graphic images also grab the attention – Leonard Sweet's work on preaching has the title *Giving Blood* (2014).

The primary focus of the research groups was on the use of an image within the model. It is important to state that the four-source model does not, of itself, require the use of an image.[2] However, my experience and the data gained by the research groups suggest that the quality of theological reflection is enriched when an image is used. The way in which each method progresses after the identification of the image is essentially the same.

The plethora of methods available for use with the four-source model can often lead to confusion and even dismay to those new to the model. Experienced mentors in the co-operative inquiry groups acknowledged that they often paid more attention to the method than the model. A deeper understanding of the model leads to greater confidence in the methods and even to the creation of new methods or steps in an existing method.

In this book and in our practice, we offer a way of mapping different versions of the four-source method in a single handout. This shows the basic shape of the model as being the same in each method; we find it easier to both comprehend and remember the methods in this way. The handout is shown as Table 2.

STEPS	TRADITION	CULTURE	EXPERIENCE			POSITION
			Personal A	Shared	Personal B	
Step 1	A piece of **Tradition** is offered for reflection	An area of **Culture** is offered for reflection	An **Experience** is offered for reflection	A shared **Experience** is identified	A personal **Experience** is identified for reflection	A **Position** statement is offered
Step 2	The passage is read out loud – people respond	The area of exploration is narrowed or refined	The story is rebuilt with shifts in action	The experience is narrowed or refined	The group explores the contribution	The group probes the statement
Step 3	The group pools its knowledge – exegesis	Is there any important information lacking?	The group and presenter agree on a shift – a slice	Is there any important information lacking?	The group contracts to work together	The group contracts to work together
Step 4	Possible statements of the heart of the matter	Possible threads or areas are identified	The presenter identifies thoughts and feelings	The group chooses one thread or issue	Thought showering leads to the heart of the matter	Thought showering leads to the heart of the matter
Step 5	The heart of the matter is chosen	The group agrees on a specific thread or area	People name similar feelings from experience	Does the thread pull on anyone's personal experience?	Does anything pull on personal experience?	Does the position pull on personal experience?
Step 6	Translate the heart of the matter into an image	Translate the thread or area into an image	Translate the feelings of step 4 into an image	Translate the thread or issue into an image	Translate the heart of the matter into an image	Translate the heart of the matter into an image
Step 7	The image is explored using the imagination					

Generating the image

[Steps]	[Tradition]	[Culture]	[Experience] Personal A	Shared	Personal B	[Position]
Step 8			**The image is interrogated using the interrogatory questions**			
Step 9	Examples of Culture are sought that are like the image		Examples of Tradition are sought that are like the world of the image			
Step 10			One example from step 9 is interrogated using the same questions as in step 8			
Step 11			The detailed answers from steps 8 and 10 are compared, looking for similarities and differences			
Step 12	Experience that speaks to the image		Examples of Culture are sought that are like the world of the image			
Step 13			Each person names the way in which their personal Position speaks to either the image or anything else touched on so far in the conversation			Individual or group Experience that speaks to the image
Step 14			Theological conversation			
Step 15			Individual and group insights			
Step 16			Implications			

A conversation between four sources

Table 2 Summary of four-source model methods

Reflection from position

Individuals and groups often have a preferred or favourite source from which to begin a theological reflection and there are many factors which might influence this decision. As individuals we are often wedded to early formative choices or influences, such as the kind of computer we first used or maintaining a hobby or pastime because of the person who intro- duced it to us. On the other hand, influential experiences may have been unhelpful, so a choice may be shaped by an uncomfortable or dissatisfying recollection. This applies equally to starting with the Position source; in my research some groups had rarely experienced this method and others revelled in it. Some of the suggestions made in this section come from the positive experience of many of the members of the Melbourne group.

In the chapter on developing theological reflection skills we will look at what insights might be gained from starting in different sources, but for now I am attaching no special significance exploring this source first. In Table 2, 'Position' is in the final column because step 12 is the same as for methods beginning from experience – this is therefore an issue of presentation rather than preference.

Position step 1

Undertaking theological reflection in a group involves a series of mini decisions, and the first one is: whose position? This is something which either the facilitator must determine before the reflection commences or which the group must discuss. Options include the facilitator suggesting a position which the group holds, or the group identifying a shared value or, perhaps the simplest of all, an individual shares a personal position. It would save group time if this individual has been approached by the facilitator sometime before the reflection began or the person concerned had volunteered at a previous meeting of the group. Let us assume a per- sonal position is offered.

Position step 2

The group begins the process of probing the statement to see if it is con- sistent with the presenter's conviction and, if necessary, it is refined or nuanced. The position is written down; questions are asked for clarifi- cation; words or terms are unpacked; and this process continues until each person understands the position statement.

A pitfall for individuals here is to permit their own position to subcon- sciously challenge the presented one; what happens in such an instance is that what appears to be a legitimate probing of the presented position is a covert attack on the presenter's position fuelled by the challenger's own strongly held position. It is not necessary for members of the group to agree with the presented statement for the group to proceed with the reflection.

Position step 3

Once the position statement is understood, individuals in the group have the opportunity, if they wish, to state the extent to which they agree or disagree with the statement. It is possible at this point to come to a group agreement around a new position statement. The group contracts to go to the next step in the reflection either by continuing with the statement offered in step 1 and refined in subsequent steps, or by agreeing to continue with a new position statement around which the group has reached consensus. Reaching a group consensus around a position statement is possible but the time taken to achieve such agreement could be considerable or the agreed group statement might be either a watered-down version of the position offered, or it might have drifted a long way from the offered position.

Position step 4

The group *thought showers* words or phrases that the position statement evokes in their thoughts and imagination. To encourage creativity and a free-flowing stream of ideas, the facilitator explains that contributions will be written up at this stage without any comment, challenge or explanation because to do so stops the flow of ideas, and there will be space to weigh the merit of each suggestion later. Adult educators have traditionally described this process as brainstorming; a thought shower is a more evocative description of this spontaneous process. The purpose of the thought shower is to eventually agree as a group what is the *heart of the matter* of the position statement. The heart of the matter is the essence or nub of the statement which has been offered and is a term coined by Patricia Killen and John de Beer (1994, 61). Inevitably this process can sometimes involve revisiting the conversation in step 2 and there may be some retracing of steps at this point. The heart of the matter might zoom in on an aspect or characteristic of the position statement as if a magnifying glass has been used which highlights a detail or it may be that a *thread* emerges. If the position statement, for example, could be compared to a necklace containing numerous beads or jewels, the magnifying glass might focus in on one of those elements, identifying that part as somehow embodying the very essence of the necklace. On the other hand, it might be that the string or wire that links the beads together captures the essence of the necklace, the thread, which holds everything together.

Ideally the phrase or thread which emerges does not contain any of the actual words or concepts of the statement but begins the process of creating *critical distance,* which is what enables a person or group to stand back from an experience sufficiently to critically reflect upon it. Gillie Bolton notes that 'In order to be critical of my own personal, social and political situation I have to be able to stand outside it to some extent' (2010, 58).

Position step 5

Individuals in the group acknowledge any powerful connections to personal experience. This is *not* the moment for individuals to begin to explore their personal experience in conversation with the offered position statement (drawing on the Experience source takes place in this method at step 13). Rather, this is an acknowledgement that in any conversation powerful processes are at work. It is an opportunity for individuals to notice within themselves if any such activity is taking place. One indication that this might be happening is a subtle or radical change in emotions or feelings. The continued attention to these emotions and feelings and the ability to manage them, either by speaking out or seeking external assistance outside the group, is all part of an individual's level of emotional competence. Often this process is connected to an event or experience in an individual's past. Sometimes it can be a collective experience. When I was working with the group in Auckland, they were aware how the context of living and working in their country affects for them the way in which they respond to any discussion related to earthquakes, and in a similar way the Brisbane group recognized how their country's experience shapes their relationship to stories or images related to flooding. One would expect a similar response to those with experience of the 11 September 2001 attacks in New York and bombings on 7 July 2005 in London, which we now refer to as 9/11 or 7/7.

At one level this step is a safeguarding issue. All theological reflection has the potential to unearth thoughts and feelings in us which we thought we had dealt with and are secure in, and surprise us by having a potency we did not expect; sometimes emotions are revealed which we did not even know we had hidden. This dynamic can be even more powerful with the four-source model. In striving not to keep our theological reflection cerebral, or in the head, the intentional drawing on both personal experience and position, coupled with the use of the imagination, adopts a more holistic, kinaesthetic approach. The internal processes at work in individuals contributes to the quality of the theological reflection taking place. There are more ways of knowing than just thinking. Our God is one who is experienced rather than simply posited, therefore the way we experience God (and for Christians, Jesus) cannot be left to rational concepts alone. It does mean, therefore, given the potential for emotional disruption (which is normal for everyone) that sometimes an individual will declare that they cannot now pursue the theological reflection because of the way in which the position chosen by the group pulls on personal experience in a way which is unhelpful. The theological reflection must stop. One cannot overemphasize the importance of this step in all the methods and it should be recognized that stopping is a characteristic of responsible and mature facilitation.

This step is not to be found in other theological reflection models, and in our experience once the principle of safety has been overtly established in this method (and experience methods), practitioners become used to routinely and carefully asking the safety question in all theological reflections they participate in. Good practice is firmly established.

Position step 6

The group translates the agreed thread or phrase into a picture or image. Examples of images are: stepping into a warm shower; being on a roller-coaster ride; watching a child take its first steps; slipping on a banana skin; yanking a dog by its lead, etc. This step is completed by drawing the image and writing the thread or phrase next to it. There may even be further consideration, to see whether the image and thread or phrase are consistent with each other. The image is now ready to be explored; see the example from the Melbourne group in Figure 9.

In the Melbourne research cycle one (2013, 4) the position statement is:

What is really valuable in EfM is that it is a community exploring who they are revealed by [or in] [the revealing] God.

This produced the image / statement:

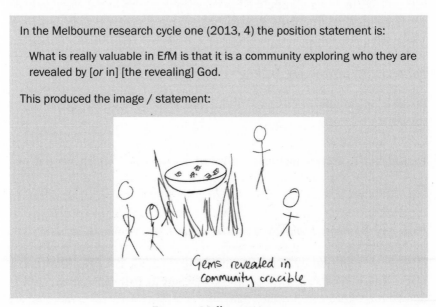

Figure 9 Melbourne image

Reflection from culture

Culture step 1

An area or aspect of culture is chosen for reflection; as in the reflection from Position above, this might come from the facilitator, an individual in the group or something the group decides together. There are two different ways in which the reflection then proceeds. If the piece of culture may be presented in an easily accessible way, such as an artefact or newspaper, the reflection follows *pathway A* in the following steps. If the area of culture presented is wider, such as a film, book, issue or section of society, then the reflection follows *pathway B*.

Pathway A culture step 2 – for an artefact

The piece of culture is examined initially by handling the object and passing it from person to person; in this way the experience is focused, narrowed or refined. A useful litmus test to check that pathway A is appropriate is the extent to which the culture may be physically touched by those present in the room.

Pathway A culture step 3

The group considers what they know about the artefact or piece of culture's provenance or source. Is the background significant? Does it change the group's understanding of the piece? What other information would be useful?

Pathway A culture step 4

Possible responses or insights about the piece of culture are thought showered.

Pathway A culture step 5

The group agrees on one suggestion from step 4A.

Pathway B culture step 2 – for a broader aspect of culture

If the part of culture that is chosen does not easily offer a physical artefact then the group thought showers statements about the aspect of culture; in this way the experience is focused, narrowed or refined.

Pathway B culture step 3

Even if step 2 suggests many avenues of exploration, the group steps back to ask if there is anything they need to know. Is any further research required?

Pathway B culture step 4

The group seeks to cluster some of the work identified in steps 2 and 3 and then proceeds to develop a statement by refining, adding to or merging statements to produce possible threads.

Pathway B culture step 5

The group produces a statement.

Culture step 6

The statement is translated into an image (see, for example, Figure 10). For a detailed description of this step see *Position step 6* above.

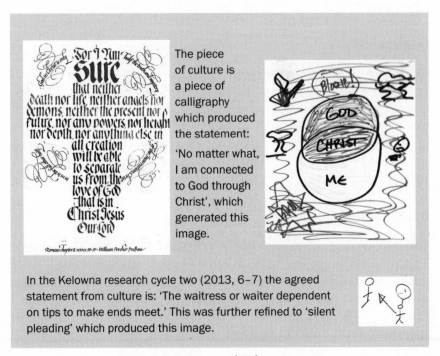

The piece of culture is a piece of calligraphy which produced the statement:

'No matter what, I am connected to God through Christ', which generated this image.

In the Kelowna research cycle two (2013, 6–7) the agreed statement from culture is: 'The waitress or waiter dependent on tips to make ends meet.' This was further refined to 'silent pleading' which produced this image.

Figure 10 Sewanee and Kelowna images

Reflection from tradition

Tradition step 1

As in the previous methods, someone from the group offers a text for reflection or the group chooses a text. This can be a favoured text, one a person finds difficult, or a 'given' text – for example, from a lectionary, or possibly a text the group has been studying academically. Scripture is an obvious choice when starting from tradition; however, anything that is part of the landscape of Christian tradition might be used, for example, a historical document such as a creed or a piece of writing from an individual or community, or a moment in history – for example, ecclesiological development or changes. If the intention is to use a passage from tradition that is unfamiliar to people, then either the presenter must come with sufficient background information or the group should be given the opportunity to conduct some research before the reflection commences or as part of step 3.

Tradition step 2

The passage is read out loud and individuals make initial responses.

Tradition step 3

The group undertakes an exegesis of the passage, pooling its resources regarding what knowledge is there about the context, author, meaning, interpretation, history of interpretation, etc. If there is no written source easily or readily available in short documentary form, then someone in the group needs to spend time researching the piece of tradition and sharing the information with the group. There is an unlimited opportunity here for research.

Tradition step 4

The group thought showers possible statements of the *heart of the matter.* This is the key point, on this occasion, for individuals or the group. Some might consider this to be the way God is speaking through the passage or the way the Holy Spirit is working. It is by pulling together personal reaction to the passage, with critical reflection through exegesis, that statements about the heart of the matter are framed.

Tradition step 5

The heart of the matter is chosen. This is not simply choosing a phrase or verse; it might be a theological statement or claim which is not overt in the text but, nevertheless, is at the heart of what the text is saying. On another day, with a different group, individuals may come to different conclusions about what this might be. Progress is made in the group by agreeing to something that works for them at that moment.

Tradition step 6

The heart of the matter is translated into an image (see, for example, Figure 11). See *Position step 6* above for a detailed description of this step.

In its third research cycle the pilot group selected Romans 8.6–11 (NRSV)

To set the mind on the flesh is death, but to set the mind on the Spirit is life and peace. For this reason, the mind that is set on the flesh is hostile to God; it does not submit to God's law – indeed it cannot, and those who are in the flesh cannot please God.

But you are not in the flesh; you are in the Spirit, since the Spirit of God dwells in you. Anyone who does not have the Spirit of Christ does not belong to him. But if Christ is in you, though the body is dead because of sin, the Spirit is life because of righteousness. If the Spirit of him who raised Jesus from the dead dwells in you, he who raised Christ from the dead will give life to your mortal bodies also through his Spirit that dwells in you.

The image generated was a rabbit in a lush field of grass.

Figure 11 Pilot group image

Reflection from experience

In this book we offer three different ways of approaching a theological reflection from experience. In the EfM community, personal experience is the source that historically has been used most frequently to generate an image; a modified version of that approach is offered in Table 2 and the steps expanded in detail below. Learning to use the four-source model is experienced by some people like learning to drive a car or swim (especially as an adult). Initially it is necessary to have a teacher and learn certain steps; there will be moments when the whole enterprise feels too complicated and you will question whether you will ever remember everything you have been taught, if you will ever actually drive or swim on your own. But then there comes a time, after you have been driving or swimming for several months, when you no longer need to 'remember' how to do it; it becomes natural and instinctive like breathing. This experience is particularly true for the first version of the reflection from experience offered here and originally known in EfM as the *microscope method* (you take a slice of experience which you examine carefully – like putting a tiny sample or sliver of tissue of something on a slide and then under a microscope). This is an extremely effective way of reflecting on experience, but it has two weaknesses. First, it takes many groups a considerable amount of time to become adept at both step 3, which involves identifying a narrow enough slice of experience, and step 4, the sifting through the thoughts and feelings of the presenter. Second, since this method involves building an image rooted in the feelings of all the members of the group, some presenters find that the theological reflection develops along lines which are much further removed from the original experience than that required by critical distance. Although such a reflection has integrity as a legitimate theological reflection, it does not often meet the needs of those seeking to use the model to reflect on specific ministerial practice.

For this reason, at All Saints we developed two variations on the method from experience: in Table 2 the reflection based upon the microscope method is named **Personal A**; the reflection on a shared experience is named **Shared**; and the second reflection based on a specific individual experience is named **Personal B**.

All three approaches are described in detail below.

Personal experience A step 1

One person in a group relates briefly an experience that puzzles them in some way, or challenges or surprises them. The incident or experience should be sufficiently worked through for the individual so that it does not cause distress to retell the story; the story must still retain some interest for the storyteller. Two minutes is a useful guide for how long the story should take to tell.

Personal experience A step 2

Initially without the presenter's help, the group rebuilds the story by identifying not every single step and detail, but the different *shifts in action* that took place. The purpose of deliberately trying to do this without help is that this encourages group listening skills and keeps the focus on the story as it is told.

The notion of a shift in action is a key concept to grasp in this method. An illustration of its meaning is that point during a film when the music changes. For example, a novelist could spend five or six pages describing how the main character walks down a busy and interesting street full of market traders, pedestrians and shoppers, but when the same scene is translated to the television screen, the style and mood of music remains the same throughout; it only changes when the character walks into a lamp-post – a shift in action! In other words, the group are not simply attempting to retell the story word for word; rather, they are looking to list the shifts in action.

Personal experience A step 3

An agreement is reached between the group and the presenter as to which shift in action will be explored. It is good practice for the group to decide this first without the aid of the presenter – this goes some way to avoiding the presenter telling the story in such a way as to focus on what they consider to be the key moment, and opens the possibility that the group will discern a key moment of which the presenter was unaware or perhaps wary. However, even if the group goes first, or is adamant in the choice of one moment, the reflection cannot continue without the overt assent of the presenter to the chosen moment or slice of the experience.

Personal experience A step 4

The presenter then shares their thoughts and feelings connected with the chosen shift in action or slice of experience. Ideally three or four different feelings are identified – if there are many feelings, three or four are given priority. It is useful to record on a flipchart the thoughts and feelings – at this stage placing them into separate columns. The culture in which some of us live, or were nurtured in, can discourage the expression of feelings (especially in some men) so sorting contributions into thoughts and feelings helps some storytellers realize they are sharing thoughts, *not* feelings.

If feelings are slow in being identified then it is sometimes possible to gently push the storyteller into trying to identify the feeling that goes with a thought; for example, 'I was thinking, that's so like him to do that' might be a thought connected with a feeling of anger or even affection – which might it be? Correctly sorting thoughts from feelings and naming them as such for the benefit of the group is a skill required of the facilitator.

Personal experience A step 5

All members of the group are asked to recall a situation in their own life when they experienced all or most of the key feelings – in this way everyone identifies with the *feelings* of the experience. The scenarios could be completely different, yet the feelings generated should be similar; note that the thoughts of the presenter are left behind.

Personal experience A step 6

The group translates the feelings identified in step four into an image or picture. See *Position step 6* above for a detailed description of this step.

Shared experience step 1

Some practitioners use case studies when teaching theological reflection. A good deal of time can be wasted discussing details or aspects of the scenario (which may not even be available) and it encourages a sense of detachment because the reflection does not involve participants emotionally. We find that starting a theological reflection from a common or shared experience is a good way round this problem, because it is based on something real and everyone can contribute. The common experience can be as simple as: what was it like getting to the group today? or something that is a part of the group's communal life – for example, last night's stormy weather. At All Saints, with students, we have, for example, used the experience of worship on the course or the experience of receiving feedback on the course – something everyone has experienced.

A reflection from a shared experience does not rely on the use of a storyteller. Telling a story is itself an acquired skill – if a group does not have any members experienced in theological reflection this can be a risky place to start because the story could be inappropriate for several reasons: too long, too emotive, or one containing unresolved personal issues.

As with other methods, the shared experience might be identified from the facilitator, an individual in the group or something the group decides together.

Shared experience step 2

The group thought showers aspects, details and questions about the context or situation; in this way the experience is focused, narrowed or refined.

Shared experience step 3

The group explores whether any important information is lacking. It either pauses and researches this information or continues after noting this gap.

Shared experience step 4

The group chooses one thread or issue.

Shared experience step 5

Does this chosen thread resonate with anyone's personal experience? If so, share briefly. This is about safety – see comments on *Position step 5*.

Shared experience step 6

The thread or issue selected in step 4 is translated into an image. See *Position step 6* above for a detailed description of this step.

Personal experience B step 1

If the reader has been carefully tracing all the steps described above on to Table 1, it will become apparent that the reflection *Personal experience B* is very similar to the reflection *Position*. The similarity is due to the contribution being personal and the group contracting to run with a theological reflection which does not necessarily ring true with their own personal experiences or position. The implication of this approach is not to be underestimated. Since the four-source model identifies position as one source which contributes to an individual's theology, a learning environment is birthed and sustained which makes it possible for people to engage in creative and supportive theological discussion with one another without having to agree with another person's position.

An experience is identified and shared by an individual in the group.

Personal experience B step 2

The group explores the story by asking questions until each person understands the key aspects of the experience which has been shared.

Personal experience B step 3

Once the experience is understood, all the members of the group check with each other that they are content to continue a theological reflection based upon the presenter's personal experience; they contract to work together.

Personal experience B step 4

The group thought showers words or phrases that the presenter's experience evokes in their thoughts and imagination, which leads to the group agreeing the heart of the matter. A detailed explanation and rationale for this process is offered above at *Position step 4*.

Personal experience B step 5

Individuals in the group acknowledge any powerful connections to personal experience. This is *not* the moment for individuals to begin to explore their personal experience in conversation with the offered position statement (drawing on the Experience source takes place in this method at step 13). Rather, this is an acknowledgement that in any conversation powerful processes are at work. Again, further detail on this process is offered above at *Position step 5*.

Position step 6

The group translates the agreed thread or phrase into a picture or image – see *Position step 6*.

Using the image to make connections

Step 7

Anyone familiar with the four-source model of theological reflection will recognize this step as being an addition to the usual way of doing a reflection. The research of the co-operative inquiry groups has revealed that even if some practitioners have been making some use of this step, the possibility for misstepping here warrants taking intentional extra care.

There are opportunities here to *refine the image*, agree on *standpoint*, and consider the *type of image* (animate or inanimate), which will provide insight to the choice of interrogatory question. This is called *orientation*.

This step does not assume or intend any doctrinal or theological exploration. The step is designed to encourage exploration of the *world* of the image. The point of this step is simply to get to know the world.

A note of caution is provided by the Melbourne group: do not read your own personal position into the picture. Pictures and images are powerful and speak to us at levels we may not always be aware of – they can stir us. Good practice for everyone at this step is to see if the image is having an impact on them – is it unearthing any emotions or pulling on personal positions?

The image generated in step 6 is drawn on a template or pattern, such as the exemplar in Figure 8; the picture is drawn in the centre together with the agreed statement. This provides an opportunity to check for consistency between the written statement and the image – has the image been drawn correctly? Does it need refining or tweaking? The issue here is not about the artistry of the cartoonist – it is about capturing the essence of the statement; see the images reproduced in this book.

Has the picture been drawn from the correct standpoint? A knack for ensuring that time and care is taken over this stage is to ask one member of the group, after exploring the image in their own mind, to describe and explain the image to another member of the group.

Having spent time refining the image to the satisfaction of the group and when everyone is agreed on the world that is being explored, the next consideration is the type of image. Is it inanimate or is it a living world? The answer to this question determines what type of interrogatory question will be used; only questions around the doctrine of creation are suitable for inanimate images; this is explored further in the next chapter.

Step 8

The image is now ready to be interrogated using theological questions. Geoff Astley has coined the phrase 'ordinary theology' to describe the different processes by which people with no formal academic education engage in what he termed 'God-talk' (2002, 1).[3] However, well before this area of theology came to be recognized as a sub-field, other theologians were championing the need to wrest theology from the confines of the academy and, as often happens with innovations, these developments were taking place in various parts of the globe in an ostensibly unrelated way. In the USA Patricia Killen and John de Beer articulate the correlational approach to theological reflection which places experience in conversation with the Christian heritage and to do this they employ theological questions which they term 'perspective' questions (1994, 135). However, to avoid what they term the use of 'religious code language', the questions are formed using simple, everyday language. In New Zealand Neil Darragh is writing about 'doing theology ourselves' and talks about using 'pivotal' questions (1995). In the UK Laurie Green is making similar claims about 'doing theology', asserting that 'all Christians worthy of the name should in fact be theologians' (1990, 7). But it is Stephen Pattison in his classic article for the *Contact* journal, 'Some Straw for the Bricks', who also in seeking to free theology from its 'dusty academic bondage' (Pattison, 2000, 137)[4] at the same time looks to the creeds as sources for theological questions:

> Christian creeds implicitly answer the questions, Where did we come from and why are we here? (*creation*), What is the purpose of human existence? (*teleology*), What stops us from attaining perfection and what would change that situation? (*evil/salvation*), In what or whom do we put our trust and what do we hope for? (*eschatology*).
>
> (2000, 141, my italics)

There does not appear to be any formal connection between the work of Patricia Killen and John de Beer and Stephen Pattison, and yet they are on the same track; asking profound theological questions using the simplest possible language.

There are decisions to be made around choosing and designing the questions and there is no correct number of interrogatory questions to ask. Experience and the research show that three is a useful number. It is partly personal choice and discernment; there is no rule for the number of interrogatory questions. Two or three questions are sufficient to begin to open the world being explored and avoids the potential bear trap of confusing four interrogatory questions with the four sources.

That being the case, the choice then is between asking one question each for three different doctrines or asking three questions about one doctrine. The art is discerning what question the image begs. The ability to design appropriate interrogatory questions requires not only an imaginative approach but also a sound knowledge of Christian doctrine and theology. There is nothing 'second class' about using the well-tried interrogatory questions for creation, sin, judgement and redemption; a facilitator or group hard pressed for time may be best advised to take this route. Typical questions might be: What would be a cause for celebration? What surprises you or stops you in your tracks? What is the wrong thing to do in this world?[5]

However, if time and resources permit, designing new questions is better, and this is explored in more detail in the next chapter.

The chosen questions are then put to the image. A knack here is to record the answers to the questions in assorted colours – this makes the process at step 11 easier to undertake.

Step 9

In this step for a reflection beginning with Tradition the group thought showers examples of culture that are like the world of the image, while reflections from all other sources would thought shower examples from tradition.

Step 10

Whichever piece of culture or tradition has been chosen in step 9 is now interrogated using the same questions as in step 8. Again, a knack here is to record the answers to the questions in assorted colours – this makes the process of step 11 easier to undertake.

Step 11

The detailed answers from step 8 and step 10 are compared, looking for similarities and differences.

Step 12

In this step, for reflections beginning from Tradition or Culture, the facilitator invites each person to identify anything in their own personal experience that resonates with the world of the image.

For reflections beginning from *Experience* or *Position* the group looks for examples in culture that are like the world of the image.

Step 13

For a reflection beginning from *Position* now is the time for individuals to share how their experience speaks to the world of the image.

For reflections beginning from *Tradition, Culture,* or *Experience*, this is the time for individuals to identify any position they hold that speaks to or against the world of the image.

Technically the position should be related to the image; however, since the principle of the four-source model is a conversation between sources, it is appropriate at this stage for individuals to speak to any position that has been engaged with at any point in the reflection. Real conversation is never sequential, and a facilitator who is pedantic about this step is likely to lose the flow of conversation.

Step 14

By now, if these steps have been generally followed and the group is operating without any unhealthy processes, the group is engaged in conversation – who knows where that will go!

Step 15

As part of the discipline of intentional conversation, at some point, before the group runs out of time, the facilitator should ask the group to identify individual or group insights gained during the reflection.

Step 16

In a similar way to step 15 the facilitator might ask what the implications for action might be for these insights, either for individuals or the group.

Steps 1 to 7 need to be followed carefully to ensure that the image which is generated does justice to the source from which it was generated. Once the interrogation of the images has begun at step 8 there can be much greater flexibility in the order of the subsequent steps or the time given to each. The four-source model is a conversation; what is important is that both individuals and the group are aware of which source they are speaking from or exploring.

Notes

1 See Frank Brown in his article 'Transfiguration: poetic metaphor and theological reflection' (Brown, 1982).

2 Killen and de Beer offer nine methods, only four of which use an image (1994, 87–110).

3 For the the way in which the field of ordinary theology has developed, see Astley and Francis (2013).

4 See note 3.

5 I am aware that this question is one that is more closely associated with moral behaviour than with the nature of sin. My experience is that people find the doctrine of sin both the trickiest to ask questions about and at the same time often the most rewarding in unlocking the nature of the world being explored. This is because this area is the most likely to draw attention to the values in the explored world which differ from the world of the person asking the questions. Asking what is the wrong thing to do in this world – e.g. when in the midst of opposition supporters at a football match, not cheering your own team is easier than asking what is the inherent debilitating condition of a football stadium or match.

4

Developing skills and understanding

GARY O'NEILL

Conceptualizing the model

One of the linguistic challenges we face when introducing people to our version of the four-source model is that we find ourselves falling back on the educational device of employing a model to describe a model. The co-operative inquiry group in Brisbane devoted a whole research cycle to playing with different ways of representing the model, exploring kinaesthetically, literally playing around with handmade models of the tetrahedron, but also asking the question: 'Why a tetrahedron?' This led to a further research cycle in which the group 'thought showered'[1] alternative models/images/pictures for the four-source model. They produced ten different pictures. When the group stood back to view their pictures, the account records something quite remarkable: silence, as they absorbed the rich imagery. One of the most powerful (and a far cry from the mechanistic tetrahedron) was the image of a vast mountain lake into which flowed four rivers. As the rivers meet, the waters swirl and swell – forming and sustaining the lake. Not only did the group accept the idea of the four-source model intellectually, they had begun to creatively play with different means of communicating the model.

This experience of the Brisbane group is important: any model is just that – a model – not reality; recognizing this fact can encourage the imagination, producing further insights. Part of the journey for each of the co-operative inquiry groups was an affirmation of the four-source model as we have presented it here: it is possible to start from any of the four sources to begin theological reflection. This is part of its strength, as it mitigates against considering the model to involve sequential steps – for some it must be experienced before it can be acknowledged.

Why so many steps?

The experience of the research helped to craft the guidance on how to use the basic model in practice as outlined in Chapter 3. A further fruit of the research was that it kick-started a process of exploration, refining and honing different elements of the model.

Both in essence, and at its simplest, the four-source model of reflection is a conversation between four sources – the model does not proscribe how much weight should be given to each source (Table 3). This is how the model was used on the induction day as described at the beginning of Chapter 1. It is similar to using steps 1, 9, 12 and 13 from the **Experience** *Personal B* column of Table 2 – that is:

1	A personal **Experience** is identified	[step 1]
2	Examples from **Tradition** are sought which speak to the experience	[step 9]
3	Examples from **Culture** are sought which speak to the experience	[step 12]
4	What personal **Position** informs the experience?	[step 13]

Table 3 Essential method – 4 steps

You will note that this simple version of the model, which we might call the essential method, does not involve the use of an image, and in this format the model and method are the same.

However, the experience and research of the authors and many practitioners indicate that the model generates richer theological insights when an image is used. Therefore, incorporating the use of an image into the method, starting with the **Experience** *Personal B* column of Table 2, might then produce Table 4.

1	A personal **Experience** is identified	[step 1]
2	Thought showering leads to the heart of the matter	[step 4]
3	Translate the heart of the matter into an image	[step 6]
4	Examples of **Tradition** are sought which are like the world of the image	[step 9]
5	Examples from **Culture** are sought which are like the world of the image	[step 12]
6	What personal **Position** speaks to the image?	[step 13]

Table 4 Using an image – 6 steps

So far, no interrogatory questions have been incorporated. The use of an image, combined with interrogatory questions, using **Experience** *Personal B* column of Table 2, produces Table 5.

1	A personal **Experience** is identified	[step 1]
2	Thought showering leads to the heart of the matter	[step 4]
3	Translate the heart of the matter into an image	[step 6]
4	The image is interrogated using the interrogatory questions	[step 8]
5	Examples of **Tradition** are sought which are like the world of the image	[step 9]
6	One example from **Tradition** is interrogated using the same questions	[step 10]
7	The detailed answers from 4 [**Experience**] and 6 [**Tradition**] are compared	[step 11]
8	Examples from **Culture** are sought which are like the world of the image	[step 12]
9	What personal **Position** speaks to the image?	[step 13]

Table 5 Using interrogatory questions – 9 steps

It is easy to see how this nine-step method quickly becomes 12 once theological conversation, individual and group insights, followed by implications are added, producing Table 6.

1	A personal **Experience** is identified	[step 1]
2	Thought showering leads to the heart of the matter	[step 4]
3	Translate the heart of the matter into an image	[step 6]
4	The image is interrogated using the interrogatory questions	[step 8]
5	Examples of **Tradition** are sought which are like the world of the image	[step 9]
6	One example from **Tradition** is interrogated using the same questions	[step 10]
7	The detailed answers from 4 [**Experience**] and 6 [**Tradition**] are compared	[step 11]
8	Examples from **Culture** are sought which are like the world of the image	[step 12]
9	What personal **Position** speaks to the image?	[step 13]
10	Theological conversation	[step 14]
11	Individual and group insights	[step 15]
12	Implications	[step 16]

Table 6 Conversation – 12 steps

It is important to stress that there is no magical, theological or praxis-inspired number of steps – the four-source model is at heart a conversation between four sources. The number of steps will depend on circumstances, not least the amount of time an individual or group can afford a theological reflection. However, what the research and experience demonstrate is that the more care and precision a group can lavish on a theological reflection, the deeper the ensuing conversation is likely to be.

1	A personal **Experience** is identified	[step 1]
2	The group explores the contribution	[step 2]
3	The group contracts to work together	[step 3]
4	Thought showering leads to the heart of the matter	[step 4]
5	Does this experience pull on personal experience?	[step 5]
6	Translate the heart of the matter into an image	[step 6]
7	The image is explored using the imagination	[step 7]
8	The image is interrogated using the interrogatory questions	[step 8]
9	Examples of **Tradition** are sought which are like the world of the image	[step 9]
10	One example from **Tradition** is interrogated using the same questions	[step 10]
11	The detailed answers from 4 [**Experience**] and 6 [**Tradition**] are compared	[step 11]
12	Examples from **Culture** are sought which are like the world of the image	[step 12]
13	What personal **Position** speaks to the image?	[step 13]
14	Theological conversation	[step 14]
15	Individual and group insights	[step 15]
16	Implications	[step 16]

Table 7 Taking care – 16 steps – at least!

In the rest of this chapter we will look at the rationale for the additional steps that have been suggested and we will quickly see that the number of steps is at one level arbitrary – it depends on how much detail or weight you imbue in a step, and that even more steps is likely to be the result of deeper thinking and exploration rather than a bureaucratic proliferation of steps. In Table 8 the steps in the method **Experience** *Personal B* are highlighted to show how that is the same as in Table 7.

Method using Experience *Personal B*

Steps	Tradition	Culture	Experience			Position
			Personal A	Shared	Personal B	
Step 1	A piece of **Tradition** is offered for reflection	An area of **Culture** is offered for reflection	An **Experience** is offered for reflection	A shared **Experience** is identified	A personal **Experience** is identified for reflection	A **Position** statement is offered
Step 2	The passage is read out loud – people respond	The area of exploration is narrowed or refined	The story is rebuilt with shifts in action	The experience is narrowed or refined	The group explores the contribution	The group probes the statement
Step 3	The group pools its knowledge – exegesis	Is there any important information lacking?	The group and presenter agree on a shift – a slice	Is there any important information lacking?	The group contracts to work together	The group contracts to work together
Step 4	Possible statements of the heart of the matter	Possible threads or areas are identified	The presenter identifies thoughts and feelings	The group chooses one thread or issue	Thought showering leads to the heart of the matter	Thought showering leads to the heart of the matter
Step 5	The heart of the matter is chosen	The group agrees on a specific thread or area	People name similar feelings from experience	Does the thread pull on anyone's personal experience?	Does anything pull on personal experience?	Does the position pull on personal experience?
Step 6	Translate the heart of the matter into an image	Translate the thread or area into an image	Translate the feelings of step 4 into an image	Translate the thread or issue into an image	Translate the heart of the matter into an image	Translate the heart of the matter into an image
Step 7	The image is *explored* using the imagination					

Generating the image

[STEPS]	[TRADITION]	[CULTURE]	[EXPERIENCE] Personal A	Shared	Personal B	[POSITION]
Step 8	The image is interrogated using the interrogatory questions					
Step 9	Examples of CULTURE are sought that are like the image	Examples of TRADITION are sought which are *like* the world of the image				
Step 10	One example from step 9 is *interrogated* using the same questions as in step 8					
Step 11	The detailed answers from steps 8 and 10 are compared looking for similarities and differences					
Step 12	EXPERIENCE which speaks to the image	Examples of CULTURE are sought which are *like* the world of the image				
Step 13	Each person names the way in which their personal POSITION speaks to either the image or anything else touched on so far in the conversation					Individual or group EXPERIENCE that speaks to the image
Step 14				Theological conversation		
Step 15				Individual and group insights		
Step 16				Implications		

A conversation between four sources

Table 8 Summary of four-source methods highlighting Experience Personal B

The richness and depth of the four-source model

Using an image

For someone reading this book to become a more skilled member of a theological reflection group, what follows in this chapter may appear to focus too much on the detailed use of the model. For those aspiring to lead a theological reflection group or to improve existing facilitation skills, this section is like taking time to look under the bonnet of the car which you are already happy driving; possibly a section for advanced drivers then!

We are going to spend some time looking at step 8 where the exploration of the image begins, but before that it is worth thinking a little more about step 7 where the image is chosen. A theological reflection group will frequently thought shower many images before proceeding to choose one. An alternative is to build on an image or let one birth another.

The Kelowna group produced an example of how to develop an image. They were beginning an exploration of the practice of tipping and were therefore starting a theological reflection from the Culture source. In exploring this in step 1, they quickly realized that this is a vast area impinging on: the tipper; the tippee; issues of justice; bribing; busking; tax laws; tip jars and more. They chose instead a slice of culture, restricting themselves to a waitress or waiter – step 5 (2013, 6–8).

In their agreed account it is significant that the group provides more detail of how the silent pleading image emerged in their critical reflection than earlier in the cycle. This implies that in the process of critically reflecting on what had happened in the research cycle the group – revisiting its work by walking through the flipchart data they recorded – saw more clearly the fine detail of the work they had accomplished together. They noted that there was:

A process of critical refinement of images which started with a begging bowl leading finally to silent pleading.

- a begging bowl   →   which led to
- hanging by a thread   →   which led to
- begging for mercy   →   which led to
- pleading for mercy   →   which led to
- silent pleading   (the eventual image)

(2013, 8)

This is a good example of how to narrow a reflection and then refine the image.

Drawing the image

Physically drawing or sketching the image, however simply, is key to the further refinement of the image and reducing the possibility of confusion. It is our experience that when a facilitator decides not to draw an image, this can sometimes lead to an unacknowledged confusion in the group – how does the facilitator know that the picture or image in each person's mind is the same? A drawn image may provide some clarity for a group. The Kelowna group, in its first research cycle, did not draw the image; I note that part way through the reflection the group account records:

> A discussion took place as to the extent the world was actually being explored from the inside and from what standpoint:[2] is anyone in the world?[3]

> (2013, 4)

Even with a group who are committed to using a theological reflection with an image there are sometimes members of the group whose personality and learning styles favour the written word. An emergent piece of good practice is to both write the agreed description of the image to be explored *and* to draw the image, as for example in Figure 12 (and note the mixture of words and sketching, for example 'lights' – there are no rules about the way we draw!).

Figure 12 Put on the spot and asked to perform

This good practice was originally identified in the Auckland group when looking for consistency between the statement and the image. They recognized the cost further down the line of an image that does not make a good fit:

The image is only ever partial and not perfect but if it misses a significant element of the statement then it has less value.

(2013, 10)

Type of image

One discussion threaded its way through the co-operative inquiry groups about animate and inanimate images. By inanimate a group would mean an image which is lifeless; the Auckland group were clear when reviewing their polished account that although they may have often used the word inanimate in conversation, technically the phrase 'non-human' more accurately describes what they mean by inanimate.[4]

The suitability of inanimate images was first explored in the pilot group when the group selected a musical instrument as the image. Culturally, the Auckland group were comfortable using inanimate images and there was some evidence of a local tradition that eschewed human images. I would take the opposite point of view because of my experience throughout my research.

A discussion ran through several sessions about the appropriateness of different types of images and possible cultural differences between the UK and New Zealand. The Auckland position was to steer clear of images that were anthropomorphic. An image of a child's first bike ride explored in the second research cycle (2013, 5) was not well received because for some people it hooked them straight into a moment in their own lives when they had watched a child on a bike. I pointed out that the images sometimes do resonate with actual experience and that is fine if the connection is acknowledged.

In the Auckland group's fourth research cycle an image of a heart monitor was generated (2013, 11). In exploring sin, the group has written: failure; the monitor cannot be fixed; power fails; there is a malfunction. My point is that the machine cannot have any control over these outcomes, so how can it be capable of sin?

One insightful outcome of the conversation on the nature of images was that in its critical reflection on its second research cycle the Auckland group recorded:

• The insistence on inanimate images does have its limitations.
• Images with people do have their pitfalls.

(2013, 7)

A cultural difference emerged between Australia and New Zealand. In the third research cycle the Brisbane group identified as a possible research question: Are dynamic images best interrogated with redemption questions and are static images best interrogated with creation theology (2013, 8)? This reveals that the members of the Brisbane group already had some experience and exploration of the *kinds* of images used in theological reflection. Sadly, for me, the group chose not to run with this question. However, in its seventh cycle the group explored an image of a five-stage water sequence; the confluence of four rivers which then fed into a lake which then overflowed (Figure 13). Initially they ran with this image as a moving image and, therefore, asked redemption/salvation questions. However, the group then realized the image was in fact a static image and therefore creation questions were required.

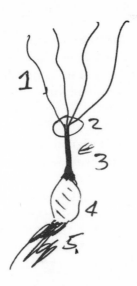

Figure 13 Five-stage water sequence

This conversation which began in the Auckland group about inanimate images, which was initially thought to stem from cultural differences, threaded its way through several co-operative inquiry groups to produce two insights. First, that both inanimate and human images are suitable for theological reflection, but that only doctrinal questions of creation are suitable for objects. Second, that moving images must be examined carefully because movement does not of itself imply life. There is a difference between moving and being moved; moving implies life and thereby choice whereas being moved is something that happens to an object by some force.

The brevity of the Brisbane agreed report does not show the depth of conversation involved here. The insight that the group reached after its critical reflection on this cycle is more representative of where the group got to eventually:

Images are not of themselves creative or redemption images; the question is: Do we use creative or redemptive ... questions to interrogate the image?

(2013, 16)

The decision a group makes on the type of image it is dealing with is important as this has implications for the type of questions that are to be used later. Deciding on the nature of the image (animate or inanimate) and its status (static or moving) is part of the process of refinement.

Standpoint

Entwined with the issue of the type of image is that of standpoint. Sewanee research cycle one (2013, 2–4) began with an old image (that is, not one created by the group that day, but one which had been used by someone in a previous theological reflection group), 'being pulled over by a police officer'. The image was drawn as in Figure 14; the group walked around the world of the image (orientation) and explored. This orientation led to a refinement of the image: the intended image is the moment at which the police officer appears at the car window.

Figure 14 Being pulled over by a police officer – external view

During the interchange that followed it became clear that one person was operating from the context of an observer on the sidewalk (he was viewing the police officer speaking with the driver as if he was *watching* the action in Figure 14). The standpoint of the image was revisited and confirmed as 'being pulled over', which led to the insight that the image needed redrawing to clearly reflect the chosen standpoint. This produced Figure 15 (a view from inside the car looking out through the car window) and it is this image that was taken forward.

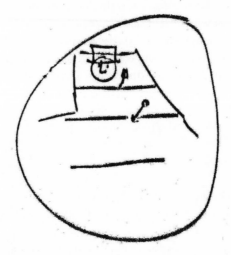

Figure 15 Being pulled over by a police officer – internal view

Completely redrawing the image in theological reflection is rare; more commonly the group decides, because of pressure of time, to carry on rather than change the image, because that is perceived as going backwards. In the Auckland group (2013, 8) even though the group realized that the image it had been exploring was not consistent with the statement that had been agreed, the group carried on.

The example of *'being pulled over by a police officer'* also highlights the significant role that language plays in a theological reflection. In the Sewanee agreed account the word 'perspective' is used consistently in both the record of the research cycle and in the critical reflection at the end of the cycle. The term 'perspective' is however one which Patricia Killen and John de Beer and EfM use to describe the questions which articulate classic doctrines or theologies. In addition, it can be used in several other ways. The Kelowna group spent part of a research cycle considering new language for old terms (2013, 13), work which formed the basis for a new glossary (see page 180). Our preferred word is now 'standpoint' and wherever possible we eschew the term 'perspective' for the sake of clarity.

The recognition of clarity (brought to the theological reflection process by the consistent use of terminology which is fit for purpose) raises the consideration of how a theological reflection is recorded. In its second research cycle the Auckland group appreciated the clarity and economy with which questions had been put and the way in which the answers were clearly written up in separate sections in different colours (2013, 7), and in Brisbane's second research cycle (2013, 6) the limitations of a reflection using a data projector were acknowledged. There is no right or wrong way to record a theological reflection, but the facilitator might ask herself if the way in which the reflection can be viewed by members of the group encourages them to hold the overview of the model in their minds. In Figure 8 those pages or sheets which are preparatory or peripheral are kept to one side so that at all times the viewer can clearly see the four sources. Writing in the answers to interrogatory questions in different quadrants with the same colour enables the process of comparing and contrasting in step 11 to take place easily.

Orientation

It is common practice in an EfM theological reflection to begin the exploration of the image by asking the question: what is the world like? However, in the Auckland group this question came to have a different purpose. In Auckland's fifth research cycle the group designed a four-step method for the exploration of an image which, as I carried this learning to consecutive co-operative inquiry groups, became known as the 'Auckland method' (2013, 14–15).

In the second step of the Auckland method, after the image has been generated, the group explores the world of the image – this might be initiated by asking the question: what is this world like? People are invited to walk around, have a look, listen, smell, etc. This step does not assume or intend any doctrinal or theological exploration. The step's purpose is to get to know the world of the image.

In undertaking this exploration, the group is doing two important things. First, it is familiarizing itself with the nature of the world. Careful consideration is required to ensure that assumptions brought from our own world are not imposed on this new world. The group asks: How does the world work? What does it look like, smell and feel like? At the same time, by undertaking this exploration together the group is simultaneously coming to an agreement about the world they are exploring. This means that when the group takes the step of asking theological questions the members of the group are, as far as possible, exploring the same world rather than different versions of it in their own mind's eye.

Only when the group is confident that it has become familiar can the members turn to interrogatory questions. The Brisbane group embraced this aspect of the Auckland method that involved exploring the world of the image and in an amazing display of succinctness simply recorded that the 'group climbed into the image' (2013, 14).

This is, I believe, what Patricia O'Connell Killen and John de Beer (1994, 22) are communicating when they write of 'entering the space of an image' (1994, 41), reproduced in Figure 16.

Figure 16 Climbing into the image

The Melbourne group developed a successful knack for ensuring that time and care is taken over the exploration of the image. One member of the group, after exploring the image in their own mind, attempts to describe and explain the image to another member of the group. This is a practical example of how the group can both explore an image and come to a consensus about the nature of the image they are exploring.

We used the term 'knack' several times in the last chapter. John Heron uses the imagery of 'heart' when trying to describe in words the essence of a knack: having the knack is the essence of a skill; it is at the heart of knowing how (1996, 111). This then is a useful term for describing how a facilitator might develop or hone their skills. Having the knack of facilitation is much more than simply learning a skill; it suggests that a person embraces a skill such that it becomes part of who they are, a way of *being* a facilitator.

A lack of orientation can lead to groups exploring a world, or image from their own world, rather than confirming that the standpoint is to be from inside the explored world. An example of this disconnect, or mis-step, can be seen in the way the Auckland group (2013, 3–5) explored the image of a koru[5] in its first research cycle. It took the group two attempts to agree on their interrogation of the work because some people were 'being' the koru while others were observing the koru.

The refining process of considering image type, standpoint, drawing and orientation do not necessarily have to occur in this precise order and a degree of shuttling back and forth may take place. However, when taken together these steps deepen the quality of the image in relationship to its generating source.

John Heron developed what he calls an 'extended epistemology' of experiential, presentational, propositional and practical knowing, summarized and developed in a chapter with Peter Reason (Heron and Reason, 2008). Although John Heron's sights are set on a loftier venture, his principle holds good for the four-source model: the experiential knowing of the chosen image, experienced by the process of orientation, becomes a presentational knowing by the drawing of the image.

Multiple images

A groundbreaking experience for me in the co-operative inquiry process was the concept of exploring more than one image simultaneously. This thread of experience began in the Melbourne group and continued in the University of the South when I participated in a training of trainers (see note 5, p. 34) event in Sewanee a few days before the Sewanee co-operative inquiry group met. In research cycle three the Melbourne group decided to explore two images generated by the group in a previous cycle: the womb, Figure 17 (the image represents the whole cycle of pregnancy in the womb), and the crucible, Figure 18. The two images were attempts to represent the E*f*M community.

An orientation of both images produced the following contrast:

small and big	*versus*	big and small
self-contained	*versus*	external input
biological	*versus*	industrial
water	*versus*	fire
self-replicating	*versus*	finite and completed
opening	*versus*	closing and concentrating

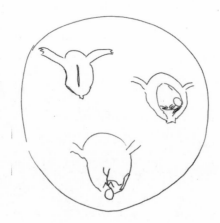

*Figure 17 E*f*M as womb*

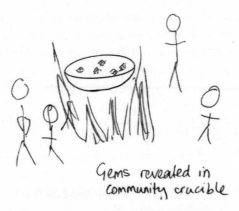

Gems revealed in community crucible

Figure 18 EfM as crucible

The group designed its own interrogatory questions based on eschatology. When the two worlds had been oriented and interrogated, comparing worlds produced:

nurturing	*versus*	clinical
non-intervention	*versus*	intervention
promise	*versus*	outcome
relationship	*versus*	product
desire	*versus*	obligation
unknown potential	*versus*	real potential
intimacy	*versus*	distance

←——————————————————

With the insight that for many people the journey in EfM is from right to left in the above list.

(2013, 10–16)

The use of two images in a theological reflection is, I believe, pioneering; although considered by practitioners in the past, it was probably deemed too complicated to handle and process. What the Melbourne group did was to handle the material with confidence and skill, producing insights that were important at a personal, national and international level for EfM; especially because EfM is a *movement* not a product (2013, 15).[6] I have not seen a multi-image theological reflection written up or referred to anywhere in the literature. The use of multiple images enables a reflection to be much more sophisticated, handling different areas of exploration simultaneously, or holding competing ideas in tension rather than favouring one avenue of exploration. This is illustrated in the next example.

The event in Sewanee was not part of my research but my participation was infused with the Melbourne experience. I was part of a group of three who offered to the event a session designed to explore the relationship between the trainers and the administrative hub at the university. The design was:

- Each person was to dream/envision what the relationship could look like.
- Images of this vision would be thought showered and three images selected to work with.
- Interrogatory questions would be designed to engage the images.
- The results would be compared.

In practice the reflection group chose four images:

A cross-functional team[7]	A dispersed intentional community
A 3-dimensional chess board	A jazz group

At the end of the reflection the group insights that were identified included:

- Surprised by the high level of discipline in all four images.
- The importance of intentionality.
- Structure is imbedded.
- EfM is a community not an organization.
- The elegance of the method used – no fussiness or repetitiveness.
- The models have a coherence.
- There is room for synchronicity.
- The images are emerging images.[8]

This concise list of astute insight and learning demonstrates how richly this multi-image method unlocked the creativity, imagination and intellect of a group of trainers with different visions of their shared international network.

Using multiple images is an effective way forward for a group that wishes to explore different scenarios or futures for a community.

Interrogating the image

The idea that doctrinal questions interrogate the image is not new; the phrase was used by the groups in Auckland (2013, 18), Brisbane (2013, 8) and Melbourne (2013, 11). From the time of the Sewanee group onwards the term 'interrogatory' question rather than 'perspective' question was preferred, marking the beginning of a change of its technical use in this research process (2013, 2).[9] I am aware that strictly speaking an interrogatory question is tautological. However, the phrase does remind the reader or the reflector that the purpose of the question is to interrogate the world or image being explored. Until a better term suggests itself I will stick with this one.

The custom and practice for training in the EfM community has been that once an image has been created the next step would be to ask questions related to Christian doctrines. In the development of EfM the primacy of these doctrines has shifted subtly over time. In Patricia O'Connell Killen and John de Beer's work their summary list is not fixed; sometimes it is creation, sin, grace and salvation (1994, 69); in their first method or process they are the nature of God, creation, sin and redemption (1994, 88); they also acknowledge that 'All Christian themes ... offer resources' (1994, 132). However, one page later they describe the classic Christian themes to be creation, sin, grace, judgement and eschatology (1994, 133). The cultural habit of EfM is manifest in the way in which theological reflection methods are displayed on the New Zealand website:

> All forms of Theological Reflection use the four-source model of understanding (Action, Tradition, Culture and Position). All also bring in the doctrinal themes of Creation, Sin, Judgment, Repentance/Redemption, although they do so in differing ways.
>
> New Zealand (2013)[10]

By 2003 Edward de Bary (2003, 145–9) had already begun to distinguish between the doctrine of creation and the doctrine of humanity, in which is included sin, judgement, repentance and redemption/salvation. Despite the written distinction between the doctrines of creation and humanity, I believe that, in practice, this separation is not made by many mentors. At best, they now have five interrogatory questions: creation, sin, judgement, grace and redemption. That is the theory, but in practice, because the pattern is so deeply rooted, the common habit is to use four questions and default to the doctrines of creation, sin, judgement and redemption.

This claim is borne out by my experience of the co-operative inquiry groups. It was rare for a group to use an interrogatory question that was not based on one of the classic four themes: creation, sin, judgement and redemption.

There were three notable exceptions: the Melbourne group used an eschatological interrogatory question in its third research cycle,[11] and the Kelowna group, also in research cycle three, used atonement (2013, 11). The boldest attempt at using a different type of question was in the Auckland group (2013, 17–19) where dominical questions were used.[12]

Choosing questions

If a wide range of interrogatory questions are to be considered, it follows that a change of practice would be required; the group would have to pause the reflection to consider which question to adopt. There is some evidence of this. In research cycle seven the Brisbane group records, 'What are appropriate interrogatory[13] questions for this image?' (2013, 14), and in the Sewanee group, in a complex research cycle two involving exploring four artefacts from culture at the same time, the group asked: 'Which theological question shall we use?' (2013, 5).

The choosing of appropriate interrogatory questions is both skilful and artful; it is important because asking questions is one of the ways in which a reflection becomes deeply theological. There is a knack in pausing the reflection, standing back and asking: What would be the best question to use here? In its critical reflection on research cycle two the Sewanee group concluded:

> The four different artefacts did indeed beg different interrogatory[14] questions.
>
> (2013, 7)

Designing questions

Asking informed and imaginative questions is one of the ways to unlock the potential of a theological reflection. Although designing questions is not new, there are no examples of the process in the literature. One example of good practice[15] is found in research cycle three of the Melbourne group which opted to use the doctrine of eschatology as an interrogatory focus and designed its own questions (2013, 12). The group concluded this part of its research cycle by producing four interrogatory questions to explore eschatology.

1 What is the stock take in this?
2 What kind of meeting of the present and future is imminent?
3 What is restless?
4 What is the opportune time?

(Melbourne, 2013, 12–13)

The ability to design appropriate interrogatory questions requires not only an imaginative approach to design but also a sound theological knowledge of Christian doctrine and theology. The members of the E*f*M co-operative inquiry groups are not academic or qualified theologians, though they are committed to developing their theological understanding. Investing time in designing interrogatory questions puts this theological formation to good use and inspires confidence, as the Melbourne group testifies in its critical reflection on research cycle three:

> This was a long research cycle and the learning was profound ...
>
> We have learned that we can come up with our own new ... questions – we need to spend time creating and sharpening tools. We need to broaden the theological and doctrinal categories that we use; ...
>
> There is no need to reinvent ... questions but there is great value in creating one's own questions.
>
> (2013, 15–16)

In its critical reflection on research cycle three the Kelowna group identi-fied the rewards of such work:

> The enriching moment was thought showering doctrinal/theological areas *before* designing those questions.
>
> (2013, 11)

The research shows that a thick (see page 34), richer, more complex the-ological reflection is achieved when time is taken to choose or design interrogative questions.

Exploring the doctrine of sin as an example of designing questions

I began to consider how to improve the use of interrogatory questions around the doctrine of sin over a decade ago. At a straightforward 'the answer is' level, the co-operative inquiry groups have done little to pro-vide a quick or easy answer. However, in its critical reflection on its first research cycle in which the group engaged with an image using different types of interrogatory question, the Kelowna group recorded:

> The point was made that writers such as Marcus Borg (2011) suggest that the language of original sin is not helpful and should be replaced by systemic [sin] or another phrase.
>
> (2013, 6)

This generated in me a process of reflective practice, in which I re-read my narrative story to see if I missed anything; read and re-read the Marcus Borg text referred to above; reviewed my own understanding of the doctrine of sin; and finally drafted some interrogatory questions that I believe begin the journey towards a better crafted engagement with the doctrine.

Marcus Borg sees a contemporary heaven-and-hell framework of Christianity that is 'sin ridden', leading, inevitably, to the theology that Jesus died for our sins.

> Recall Mel Gibson's blockbuster movie *The Passion of the Christ*. It focused on the last twelve hours of Jesus's life, from his arrest through his torture, suffering and death, and portrayed all of this as Jesus bearing the sins of the world. Recall its enthusiastic reception by many conservative Christians. Even Pope John Paul II endorsed it; he said, 'It is as it was.' The message was clear that what matters most about Jesus is his death as a substitutionary sacrifice for the sins of the world.
>
> Sin needs to be demoted from its status as *the* dominant Christian metaphor for what's wrong among us. As noted above, it is not the only biblical image for the human condition, not the most important one, not even a first among equals.
>
> (2011, 13 and 144)

I am favouring the work of Marcus Borg here because the intention of his book *Speaking Christian* is an attempt to give a contemporary understanding to traditional Christian words and he does so without resorting to technical language – this is a good place to quarry material for designing interrogatory questions.

As I read Marcus Borg I note that the biblical images for the human condition (sin) that he refers to include:

- Slavery
- Exile
- Lacking a path of return
- Infirmity
- Blindness[16]
- Hubris
- Sloth
- Idolatry

I wonder what thought-showered questions might begin to pick at the essence of some of these images, for example:

- Who or what is ruled in this world? By whom or what?
- In what ways are the inhabitants of this world wounded? Who is wounding? Who is being wounded?
- Who or what is 'held' in this world? Who or what 'holds'?
- Who or what aspires to place themselves at the centre of this world?
- What connections existed that have now been lost?

The work of exile resonates with the work of Walter Brueggemann (1978, 1986, 1997, 2012) in which he imagines what it is like to speak of and preach to those in exile. Drawing on his work, Michael Frost explores dangerous memories that will sustain twenty-first-century exiles before moving on to consider promises and critiques (2006).

This adds grist to the mill for my thought shower and suggests further questions:

- What is dangerous in this world?
- What songs do people sing in this world?
- What is promised?

In my experience the use of an interrogatory question around the doctrine of sin often produces the most confusion in a group; the group itself may not be aware of this confusion, but the observer or skilled facilitator would notice that the answers the group gives to the question are not consistent with one another – in other words, each member of the group has a different understanding of what sin is.

One way to mitigate this confusion would be to engage in an intentional, disciplined, informed, yet imaginative and playful, discussion on the nature of sin and then attempt to design interrogatory questions. I offer the questions suggested above, inspired by Borg, Brueggemann and Frost, as a catalyst to such conversations and designs.

There are some examples of interrogatory questions in Table 9.

WHOLENESS [Creation]	BROKENNESS [Sin]	RECOGNITION [Judgement]	REORIENTATION [Repentance]	RESTORATION [Salvation]
What reveals the goodness in this world?	What is distorted in this world?	What brings you up short in this world?	What might you turn away from?	Who or what could fulfil the promise of this world?
What is most attractive in this world?	What is the wrong thing to do in this world?	What takes you by surprise in this world?	What might you turn towards?	What would complete this world?
What holds this world together?	What obscures us from the truth?	What causes a crisis?	What risks must be confronted?	What breathes life into this world?
What reveals the character of this world?	What is unseen, unheard, or intangible?	Who or what do we need to remember in this world?	What brings insight in this world?	What is a source of hope in this world?
What is the source of life in this world?	What inhibits sensing (e.g. touching, tasting, etc.) in this world?	What takes your breath away?	What needs to die so something can live?	What is the cause of celebration in this world?
What do we encounter in this world?	Who suffers in this world?	What holds up a mirror to you?	What is the source of healing?	What is the source of new life in this world?
What is valued most in this world?	Who or what creates barriers in this world?	Does a sense of self override a sense of others?	What shifts the course of this world?	Where is hope?
What holds this world together?	Who or what is forgotten in this world?	Who or what makes the prophetic voice in this world?	What still holds you back in this world?	Where is grace?
Who decides in this world?	Who or what is a cause of estrangement in this world?	Who or what causes potential to be stifled in this world?	How would this world be redeemed?	Where is glory?
Who benefits in this world?	Who or what is seductive in this world?	Where is conversion needed?		What restores or brings balance to this world?
				What brings new life to this world?

These were designed by Judith Evans and Christopher Halliday in October 2016 and subsequently modified by the editor.

Table 9 Sample interrogatory questions

Further research

At the end of research cycle five on models, the Brisbane group posed the question (of the models): Where is the Holy Spirit in these models (2013, 12)? Laurie Green cites the Holy Spirit as the inspiration for imaginative links between life and faith (2009, 15), suggesting that theological reflection requires openness to the Spirit (2009, 24), but apart from the acknowledgement that the imagination may be open to the Holy Spirit in times of quiet contemplation (2009, 175) he is never clear how this actually happens.

In research cycle three the Kelowna group (2013, 8) completed a reflection which, when mapped out, produced Figure 19. The 'spaces' created by the reflection were identified in the critical reflection at the end of the cycle. There is something quite remarkable and beautiful about the way in which this scripted theological reflection demonstrates the points made in the group's learning from cycle three. The precise interrogation questions had led to concise answers, and to the insight, illustrated by the *spaces*, that theological reflection is a process that moves in time and space. Theological reflection is taking place in both the group and in individuals, even when no one is speaking. Perhaps this is an illustration of one of the ways in which the Holy Spirit works – in the gaps. Gillie Bolton would say that

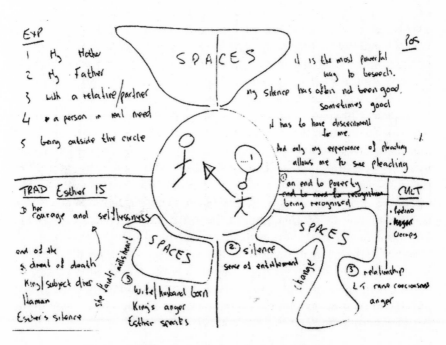

Figure 19 Kelowna research cycle three: reflection map

if practice is an art then reflection on it is artistic.[17] The spaces in Figure 19 have their own beauty and resonate with Kathryn Tanner: 'The Holy Spirit moves over the surface of the waters and not in their depths' (1997, 162).

Norms and ground rules[18]

In their critical reflection on a third research cycle the Brisbane group identified a group dynamic which questions the extent to which the facilitator needs to know if the image can be questioned or clarified (2013, 7). At first this appears to be a question about refining or clarifying when, in fact, it is an issue about a group norm.

For effective learning to take place the facilitator needs either to have agreed some ground rules for the group before the theological reflection, or to be confident that they understand correctly what the current group norms are regarding contributions from individuals. Group norms are frequently invisible (Napier and Gershenfeld, 1999, 111) and groups are often reluctant to talk about them. Confusion between group norms and ground rules often arises. Ground rules are agreements which a new group provisionally agrees at the beginning of its life, whereas in the field of group process, norms emerge during the life of the group; they are sometimes subconscious, but they provide important data for a skilful facilitator. Cultural differences can confuse the way in which we approach norms – in the USA is it just a translation issue that when someone says 'norms', what they really mean (to English ears) are 'ground rules', or is the early setting of norms sometimes an attempt to control?[19]

In some Christian contexts, it is often considered inappropriate or uncaring to question the contribution of an individual – this results from a misunderstanding of the concept of pastoral care. In order to affirm all members of a group those facilitating the group are often encouraged to write up everything that is said so that people do not feel left out. The weakness of this approach is evident when a contribution is made which is either inaccurate or unhelpful. In this situation, the facilitator needs to know whether a contribution from an individual may be challenged or modified. If the group norm is to be pastoral and caring to people, it makes it difficult for the facilitator to encourage a norm of critical reflection.

An emerging norm which in some ways surprised me (because it was unspoken?) was the assumption about worship. The agreed account of the Auckland group begins:

The three days of this co-operative inquiry group was rooted in a daily pattern of prayer and worship consisting of morning prayer, midday eucharist and night prayer; presided over by a member of the group acting as chaplain.

(Auckland, 2013, 1)

I realized after the event the importance of the worship both for me as the researcher and the group. A firm arrangement had been put in place for one trainer to act as chaplain to the training event. This meant that the worship for the co-operative inquiry group, operating within the parameters of the wider event, was already planned and agreed. On what were very full and demanding days, the inquiry group was called to worship three times a day. On one day, the call was literal – we were reminded that the session had ended, and worship was about to begin. For a group focused on the *mechanics* of theological reflection, regular worship reminds individuals of the reality of their faith and encourages theological reflection to be an exploration and worship of the divine rather than a task to be completed.

Some co-operative inquiry groups threaded the worship and the work of the group together, as illustrated by the Melbourne account. At the beginning of cycle two the mentors invited the group, 'in a few moments of worshipful silence', to identify a memorable moment from an EfM group, which would kick-start the research cycle, and at the end of that same session the worship leaders invited members to focus on the image that had been produced during the cycle and what they would take away from it (2013, 7 and 10).

The research data underlines the importance of an inquiry group making time for the building of community, establishing ground rules and monitoring the emergence of group norms. Once the learning community has been established it turns to its task as a theological reflection group.

The first data that the co-operative inquiry groups furnished was that they worked. The initial anxiety that the groups might either not form or, having formed, might proceed along lines which would have been unhelpful to this research, simply did not materialize. Differences in culture were noted but did not play a major part in the life of any group. No group existed in a vacuum – each was subject to processes flowing from its geographical, political and social setting – where necessary, these process issues were addressed in order not to limit the quality of the learning environment created in each group.

Starting from different sources

At the heart of the four-source model, as we are presenting it in this book, is a conversation between four sources. We are not suggesting that undue weight should be given to any source or sources; in fact, discerning as an individual or a group your habitual tendency to favour a source is an important indicator to your own theological position. However, what research and experience does suggest is that if an ongoing theological reflection group intentionally ensures a balance of reflections initiated over a period of time from all four sources, the group is more likely to consider giving appropriate weight to each of the sources. Again, this is not to suggest that the four sources should be given equal weight, but that those engaged in theological reflection should be aware of how much weight they are assigning to each of the individual sources. It may be that many theological reflection groups do not sufficiently understand either the importance of the position source or the assumptions that they are making, either individually or corporately, about the weight given to that source. An examination by individuals or a group of the weight and importance that they attach to each source is, in fact, important data that offers insights into the positions that the groups or individuals hold, but did not realize they held.[20]

Part of the journey for each of the co-operative inquiry groups was an affirmation of the four-source model as I had presented it and that it is possible to start from any of the four sources and generate an image.

> The group reaffirmed its faith in the four-source model and the value of using an image every time we want to make a connection between sources.
>
> Auckland (2013, 11)

This is part of its strength, as it mitigates against considering the model to involve sequential steps – for some it must be experienced before it can be acknowledged.

Notes

1 See the Glossary.

2 In the agreed account the word 'perspective' is used at this point; and see note 41.

3 Generally agreed accounts are not changed but for consistency I do change 'perspective' to 'standpoint' when that is implied and 'perspective' to 'interrogatory' as required – see note 9.

4 *The Shorter Oxford English Dictionary* (1972), for example, defines inanimate as 'not animated or alive; destitute of life, lifeless; *spec.* not endowed with animal life, as in inanimate'.

5 The koru, which is often used in Māori art as a symbol of creation, is based on the shape of an unfurling fern frond. Its circular shape conveys the idea of perpetual movement, and its inward coil suggests a return to the point of origin. The koru therefore symbolizes the way in which life both changes and stays the same. Source: Royal, 2009.

6 The influential forces of economics, power, control and reputation mean that the way this insight is received will vary considerably in different parts of the worldwide EfM community. The two polar extreme contexts might be the difference between a small independent charity run by volunteers in the UK and a multi-million-dollar operation in the USA with employees to consider and relationships with both a powerful university and episcopal dioceses.

7 A cross-functional team is a group of people with different levels of skill, expertise and seniority working towards one goal. The context envisioned here was medical.

8 The quotes here are not from any agreed account. The reflection was written up as it progressed by the use of flipchart paper. After the end of the reflection the group of trainers gave me permission to photograph the wall of paper to use as an example in my research.

9 For the sake of consistency, the term 'interrogatory' is used throughout rather than 'perspective'. When drawing on a co-operative inquiry group which uses the term 'perspective', rather than change the word, it is simply omitted, and an ellipsis used to alert the reader.

10 This juxtaposition of four sources (Action, Tradition, Culture and Position) with four doctrinal themes illustrates how easy it is for the novice learner to confuse sources and themes.

11 Part of that research cycle is reproduced on page 80.

12 The eucharistic acts of Jesus in taking, blessing, breaking and sharing bread, famously identified in the work of Dom Gregory Dix (1945). The group asked 'What is taken, thanked, broken, given away?' in the world being explored.

13 See note 9.

14 My note: see note 9.

15 Others examples are: Auckland (2013, 14); Kelowna (2013, 9); Sewanee (2013, 6).

16 I instinctively shy away from this image because I think it is too imbued with both traditional Christian and contemporary baggage. See John Hull (2001).

17 See the poem she quotes, 'Mind the Gap' (2010, xvi).

18 For a discussion of norms, see Rodney Napier and Matti Gershenfeld (1999, Chapter 3).

19 Napier and Gershenfeld (1999, 120) call this social influence.

20 One way to achieve this would be by using Johari's window – practitioners may discover that the area showing what we do not know about ourselves is larger than expected (Chambers, 2002, 111–12).

PART TWO

Theological Reflection in Practice

5

Teaching biblical studies

LIZ SHERCLIFF

As the title suggests, this chapter will mainly be of interest to those who teach biblical studies in one form or another. While there is an academic bias in it, there are also useful ideas for those who lead home groups.

Biblical studies is a broad field, and for the purposes of this chapter I need to specify my meaning. Academically, I have taught a range of what are loosely termed 'biblical studies modules' over the past few years, ranging from introductions to both Old and New Testaments, to thematic exploration of biblical themes. I have also been a member of, and led, what might be considered informal biblical studies groups, in the form of home groups, Lent groups and other church-based study forums.

No matter the focus, nor indeed the assessment method, the Bible has been handled in a broadly similar way: read the given passage; think about what it might mean; go to other authorities. In the academic context these authorities might take the form of commentaries. In parish groups it might simply be the previous Sunday's sermon. At this point, it might cynically be suggested that whatever group members first thought the text said, this is now abandoned in favour of the commentator's interpretation.

Every passage of Scripture is freighted both with religious and socio-political history, and with personal devotional meaning. Rarely is there any direct correlation between the two. Neither one, alone, can render the full potential meaning of a Bible passage. Where the tendency is to empha-size 'expert' opinion, the devotional is lost, and the meaning distanced from today. Where the personal reading is emphasized the wisdom of tradition is lost. If our teaching is to encourage holistic biblical interpre-tation, then whether we lead in the classroom or the home group we need a way of handling the Bible that can bring out both types of meaning. Using the sources of Experience and Position can balance out the strong forces of Tradition when we come to biblical text. Informed Tradition can balance out over-emotional responses to devotional readings.

What kind of biblical student?

The way in which people study the Bible is often set by the context in which they do so. A home group might start with refreshments, sit as a group in comfortable seats in someone's home looking at and speaking to one another. Apart from the group leader, most might have nothing more before them than the Bible. A class group is more likely to sit behind desks, have notebooks or computers before them, look towards the front of the room and speak through the adjudication of a tutor. The seating arrangement alone establishes at least one aspect of group culture. In the circle, everyone has a voice. In the class, the tutor is in control – even if desks and chairs are arranged in a horseshoe!

In a home group, no matter what the aspirations of the group or church leader, people arrive with their own agendas – friendship, fellowship, faith building. Hence a common frustration is 'we never got to the point' – caused at least in part because a group agenda is never clarified. In class, the aims are likely to be more common – learn what is needed for assessment, perhaps, and the agenda determined by the person in control. Yet the classroom might contain more disparate views than a group of people from the same church.

Often, by default, it happens that in a home group the Bible is read devotionally, while in the classroom it is read academically. For effective study of the Bible both are essential. Particularly where classroom learning is aimed at developing effective ministers of the word, academic learning alone is not enough. Tradition and personal experience need to be in tension. For that to happen a classroom culture in which students are comfortable to explore both the works of great scholars and their own readings of a passage needs to be intentionally created.

Furniture arrangement is, of course, influential. But perhaps the most effective way of creating culture conducive to holistic Bible study is willingness on the part of the tutor to relinquish the safety of the distance created by speaking from academic authority, and to speak first from personal experience.

Living faith as inquiry

Beginning with Experience dispels the illusion that academic biblical studies can be objective. It foregrounds the concept that however I read the Bible, my reading will always be influenced by myself, my lived faith. At its best, it encourages others to live faith as inquiry too, to see the Bible not only as a historical document, but also a living one. It places in high regard all faith experiences present in the room, not just that of the educator. It becomes apparent that the tutor themselves was once somewhere else, and will soon be in a different place again, because inquiry moves things on.

So, rather than begin with a genre, or writer, or theme, biblical studies classes might begin with exploration of a text. The whole group might discuss their reactions to it. Personal Positions might be named. Through this process the text lives.

In a biblical studies class I then go on to consider Tradition. How has the text been read by the Church in the past? What do commentators say? Often there will be similarities between the 'experiential' and the academic readings so that key ideas can be drawn out. Finally, the key ideas might be related to contemporary or church culture.

It is possible to begin the study of a text from outside the text itself. The well-known photograph of a Sandinista militia woman nursing her baby while carrying a gun is a good way of starting a study of the Magnificat, for example.

In this session I simply showed the picture on screen and discussed what students saw in it. I gradually fed in some background information, such as where and when the photo was taken. Then, without too much comment, we went on to read the words of Mary in Luke 1. Such a session could then go on to discuss parallels between Mary's words and those of Jesus in Luke 4.18, 19; or Luke's soteriology; or liberation theology.

Similarly, a session on apocalyptic writings could begin with Picasso's *Guernica*. In my experience, few students know the picture and so work to decipher it might provide a starting point. Ideas that abstract art can describe truth can be carried over into interpretations of parts of Revelation, Daniel, or Ezekiel.

Academic devotional teaching

I recently taught a short biblical studies module over a few days at a summer school. It was called 'Methods of Reading the Bible'. The recommended texts for the module dealt with source analysis, narrative theory, literary criticism, form analysis, redaction history, in fact all the usual suspects including even some liberation theology. But as I thought about the students and the ministry for which they were being formed, I felt that the traditional approach to biblical studies was insufficient by itself. After all, it is unlikely that form criticism would be of use in pastoral work, nor source analysis in mission, nor yet redaction history in a Sunday sermon. What most congregants want of their minister is the ability to handle the Bible as though it still speaks. I decided that in this module we would explore both academic and devotional Bible reading, including personal and group study. Rather than read about reading the Bible, we would actually read the Bible.

First, I tried to create as appropriate an environment as possible. I rearranged the classroom seating into a horseshoe so that students could speak to one another without having to go through me. I removed flip-charts and switched off screens.

Each session began with some kind of devotional reading, broadly modelling a range of Church tradition. The idea was not that this was a worshipful start to the session, but that it *was* the session. We spent a quarter to a third of each session in devotional reading. The range of methods included meditative reading,[1] a group Bible study,[2] focusing on one verse,[3] a dwelling in the word session,[4] and a lectio divina.

In the next third of the session we discussed different approaches to biblical criticism: reader response, literary and canonical, feminist, liberationist, historical-critical. Having enjoyed a privileged position in biblical studies for so long, the placement of historical-critical was intentional. For the final third of each session we returned to the Bible, and read a selected passage from the perspective just discussed.

The structure of the sessions did not overtly acknowledge four sources of theological reflection. The aim was simply to move the reading of the Bible from a theological activity to a place where personal experience and theological thinking interact. Although the sessions began with an experiential reading of Scripture, biblical interpretation did not necessarily start there. The Bible could be interpreted in the light of experience but, equally, experience could be read in the light of Scripture.

Essential to the module was that students understood who they were when they came to the Bible. A couple of weeks beforehand I sent out a 'Personal Inventory' questionnaire and asked students to complete it (see Table 10).

Personal inventory for understanding biblical interpretation

In light of this inventory, we read the story of Ruth, and asked in what ways we were like or unlike her. The exercise brought new insight to the story. For most, this was the first realization that many of us have more in common with Boaz, and even Naomi, than with Ruth. We then linked this work to a socio-political reading of the story, contemplating the idea that the story may have been written at the time of Ezra and Nehemiah – the story of a Moabite refugee, among the Israelites, at a time of ethnic cleansing. Read culturally there seemed to be much of direct relevance in the story.

In another session, rather than examining how we came to the text, we looked for ourselves in the text – in other words, we read the text devotionally and considered what it might have to say to us. On this occasion the passage used was Genesis 28.10–22, the story of Jacob's dream. Rather than linking a previous experience to the passage, in this reading we were experiencing the narrative itself. Despite working as a group, the range of experiences was wide.

Gender	How does your gender identification relate with that of the dominant culture? The same? Different? Is this problematic?
	Is your gender location an advantage, or a disadvantage?
Culture/ Ethnicity	Are you a member of a dominant culture? Is this an advantage/ disadvantage?
	Are you bicultural? Do you consider this an advantage/ disadvantage? What is your preferred culture?
	Is your cultural location an advantage/disadvantage?
Race	Are you a member of a dominant race? A marginal race? An oppressed race?
	Is your racial identity an advantage/disadvantage?
Class	Into which economic class were you born? Are you in the same class today?
	Have you ever belonged to an invisible class (e.g. displaced, un- or underemployed, disabled, etc.)?
	Has your education improved your class standing?
	Is your class location an advantage/disadvantage?
Religion	Were you raised in a religious tradition? What did that tradition teach you about interpretation of the Bible?
	Are you presently participating in a religious tradition? How does that tradition make use of the Bible?
	Are you a member of the dominant religious group? Of a religious minority?
	Is your religious location an advantage/disadvantage?

Based on Diane Bergant in Mark Roncace (Roncace and Gray, 2012, 16)

Table 10 Personal inventory

A historical-critical method was used when reading the well-known parable about sheep and goats from Matthew 25. Rather than engage in a theological debate about judgement, we began the session by exploring the cultural context in which Matthew wrote. Jerusalem had fallen, the Temple was destroyed, many Jews, including Jesus' followers, had fled. Why, at a time when judgement had obviously already come, did Matthew include in his Gospel for this church at this time a message about feeding the hungry?

Teaching method

Classroom practice informed by a four-source model of theological reflection readily acknowledges the experience existent in the room. The tutor is no longer the 'sage on the stage', it is not their job to deposit knowledge into the heads of their students, the knowledge-making process is communal. This requires careful planning on the part of the tutor, because rather than control discussion so that what they already know is brought up, the class could go in several directions, for which they need to be prepared.

A key strength of the four-source model for teaching is its lack of susceptibility to binary thinking. Where traditional methods easily degenerate into the kind of two-sided debate where each thinks they need to defend a position from the other, the four-source model asserts the relevance of perspective, and lived experience. Equally, uncritical sharing is avoided while the process used to arrive at convictions is analysed. A direct impact of this on biblical studies will be that argument and reasoning will no longer be privileged, thus undermining dominant groups and traditions. Disparate and even discordant approaches to life and faith will prove to be enriching.

As we have seen, an early task is enabling students to identify their own subjectivity and the norms that have helped form them. This facilitates authentic, devotional reading of the text as well as appropriate critical dialogue with it. Such learning should prove liberating for both the Bible and its readers. Readers will see beyond the pervasiveness of traditional exegetical approaches to new possibilities, including assumptions that all texts must make sense.

Teaching biblical studies using four sources of theological reflection requires a careful balance between planning teaching and simply allowing for learning. The teaching session overview might resemble a mind map rather than a lesson plan, with key points divided under the four headings (Tradition, Culture, Experience, Position). These might be presented in quadrants on the planning document, rather than in a list, so that the session can start at any point, and move freely between them. Feedback can be recorded on a flipchart in quadrants. Rather than the image used in more 'free flow' theological reflections, I usually record my learning aim in the centre space (see Figure 20).

Particularly for the Tradition and Culture sections I have learning materials that will extend students' learning and add to their contributions. Often there are additional materials for the other quadrants too, such as the Personal Inventory (Table 10).

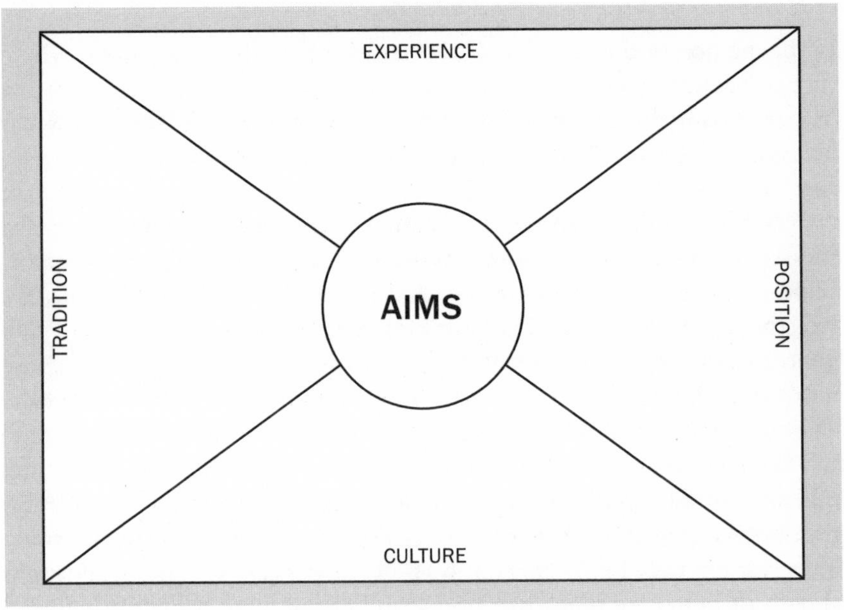

Figure 20 Aims and sources

There are various means of recording what are called 'insights' in a theological reflection exercise. Often all that is needed is five minutes at the end of the session in which students can record their own learning in a learning journal. Other helpful activities are 'gem, rock, grit' or 'going, staying'. In the first, I give students a sheet with three columns, as in Table 11.

Gem	Rock	Grit

Table 11 Insights

In the 'Gem' column they are invited to record what they have found valuable in the session, for any reason. 'Rock' is something they didn't find helpful, or struggled with. 'Grit' is something that irritated them, and they intend to work with, like the grit in an oyster. In 'going, staying' they record two things they want to take with them at the end of the session, and two things they want to leave behind in the classroom.

Assessing learning

In the method outlined above, it is often true that the tutor knows where they are going and is confident they will get there, but has no idea how. Yet professionally, at the end of every session, tutors need to know what learning has taken place. Feedback from the exercises mentioned above can be helpful here.

Perhaps a more pertinent question is whether learning through a four-source model of theological reflection can be assessed effectively in biblical studies. I want to suggest that it can. When the process works effectively a fuller exegesis of any Bible passage can be reached, which almost inevitably includes what it might say for today's Church. Using the method students avoid the exegesis–application model of biblical study. They are able to deal with the Bible as both a historic and living word.

The focus on Tradition involves commentary work, as with a traditional biblical studies assignment. Culture delineates the validity of interpretation by acknowledging that the passage seems to mean a particular thing in a given context. Experience shows how the passage lives today. Position should form part of the conclusion – 'in light of what has gone before, I believe the passage to mean …'

Notes

1 This involved three stages: notice the details of the passage; identify the essential themes; think about how it might apply personally.
2 Based on Whitney Kuniholm (2010).
3 Taken from an article I wrote for the Diocesan Prayer Diary.
4 Pat Taylor Ellison and Patrick Kiefert (2011).

6

Theological reflection and exegesis

LIZ SHERCLIFF

Approaching the New Testament reflectively

In this chapter I explore how the four sources of theological reflection might be used in biblical exegesis. I describe the process from my own experience, because elsewhere in this book there are examples of group work. I begin with an exegesis starting from Position. I then move to an example that began from Culture within the Church, with some comment on reference to wider culture. No example constitutes a complete exegesis, but serves simply to illustrate how using the four sources of theological reflection might lead to new insight.

Position

I remember one particular sermon very clearly, because I struggled hard. Here was I, by no means a convinced royalist, having to preach on the Feast of Christ the King. I was familiar with a range of hymns and worship songs extolling an apparently combative Jesus, but did not find them appealing.

That summer the nation had celebrated the Jubilee of Queen Elizabeth II – not a powerful, conquering hero but by now (it seemed to me) a frail, if accomplished, elderly woman. Awareness of international news led me to believe that for large swathes of our planet being ruled by a 'king' was by no means a positive experience. And, come to think of it, most kings in the Bible also left a great deal to be desired. I was distinctly uncomfortable at the prospect of preaching about a concept of kingship in which I did not believe. Clearly my personal position was going to get in the way of my preaching unless I could resolve the issue.

I quickly discovered there was also a lack of tradition around the feast. It is a recent addition to the Church's calendar, having been introduced in 1925 by Pope Pius XI, and adopted into the wider Church along with the Revised Common Lectionary towards the end of the twentieth century.

I did what I often do when I get stuck with the exegesis of a passage. I went for a walk. By the time I got home, I had two options: withdraw from the preaching slot, or work out what the Bible means when it refers to Jesus as 'King'.

Tradition

Exploring the biblical Tradition cast some light on the subject. God is not called King in the Old Testament until after the Israelites had a human king. Giving God the title was making the divine in human image, an extension of the human concept. In the New Testament, despite the fact that it is impossible to read any of the Gospels without encountering the kingdom, Jesus is rarely referred to as King. Clearly, if he is a king, it is of a very different kind.

As often happens in theological reflection, the interaction of two sources, in this case Position and Tradition, led to an insight about the passage I was to preach on.

The Gospel reading was John 18.28–38, the story of Jesus before Pilate. My uncertainty about what was meant by kingship in the context of Jesus' life had been very similar to that of Pilate, 2,000 years ago. Just as I had not understood, nor had he. I had been asking of Jesus '*are* you the King?', just as Pilate does in the passage. This insight led to a new empathy with Pilate, a new understanding of how challenging the person of Jesus was and is.

Examining the passage from the gospel tradition, it began to seem clear that the writer of John has been setting up this scene all along. He began the whole thing by saying: 'In the beginning was the Word, the Word was with God and the Word was God.' This kingdom didn't begin with Abraham, Moses or the prophets as the Jews might have expected. It began right at the beginning. Just as Jesus says to Pilate that he has come to declare the truth, so John said right at the outset that the true light that gives light to everyone was coming into the world. And as is so obvious now, before Pilate: 'The light shines in the darkness but the darkness has not understood it.' In this passage John brings the clash of kingdoms to a climax.

In this example, recognizing my own position with regard to kingship led to a (for me) new interpretation of the passage. Ultimately, it led to new insight into the actions and attitudes of Pilate, the man it is so easy to blame, but who was probably as confused as I was by Jesus' radical kingdom.

Researching the tradition of kings in the Old and New Testaments liberated me from the kind of kingship that discomfited me.

Culture

In the end it was this dissonance between commonly held views and new insights that became central to my sermon. I needed, therefore, to find in culture a means of connecting with it. In the end I chose two linked examples, one of which would certainly no longer work. This is how I began:

> Apparently my world has undergone a dramatic change. Until recently my mobile service was provided by Orange. But now it's provided by EE. Just seeing EE appear on my screen makes me want to edit it to say EE By Gum. But that's not the point. Whereas before I could use my phone to contact whoever I wanted now I am part of a whole new world.
>
> I am connected with Everything Everywhere. And if you have seen the advert I am also connected with Everyone. I now live in an Everyone Everything Everywhere age.
>
> It would all be well beyond the conception of my grandmother, who didn't even have a landline until she was in her seventies and even then had to be reminded that an operator wouldn't be asking who she wanted to speak to when she picked up the handset!
>
> Seeing Christ as a King involved a similar gap of understanding for Pilate, for the religious leaders, for the ordinary person in the Galilean street and for his disciples.

Recognizing the heart of my exegesis and finding in culture an idea that resonated with it provided an effective analogy. In fact there are two comparisons made, a contemporary one with an advertisement on television at the time – an analogy that would not work once the advertisement had been succeeded by the next; and one that would resonate with many present, and actually has greater longevity.

Starting exegesis from Christian culture

We live in a culture where strength is valued, we are supposed to overcome difficulties, shine in the face of adversity, dance in the rain. It makes little difference whether we consider the culture in church or that of the wider world. In church 'Our God reigns'; Christian soldiers march onward; 'I believe'. It is no wonder therefore that we often interpret biblical stories from the perspective of strength – at least, from the perspective of male strength. One such example is the story of Philip and the eunuch (Acts 8.26–40).

Philip is a hero of the faith, obedient to God, reads the situation well, interprets Scripture and makes a convert. Most exegetes, therefore, place obedience, mission, or reliance on the Spirit at the centre of the story, making it one which can easily make readers feel inadequate.

The eunuch, on the other hand, is largely ignored. He was returning to his own land, not one that features in New Testament writings. He was on the road out of Jerusalem, away from the locus of the Church. As a human being he was regarded as defective. Since a future was guaranteed through the parenting of children, he had no future. He would have no heirs, so no need to embezzle funds from the queen; he was a eunuch so could be trusted with the royal harem. His main identity came from what he lacked.

He was, of course, reading the Scriptures when Philip was brought alongside his chariot. Because of our cultural focus on strength, it's easy to miss what he was reading. The God we most easily identify in the passage is the one who miraculously ferries Philip to this divine appointment. But perhaps the God who drew the eunuch through this passage was quite different – the lamb who had no future:

Like a sheep he was led to the slaughter,
and like a lamb silent before its shearer,
so he does not open his mouth.
In his humiliation justice was denied him.
Who can describe his generation?
For his life is taken away from the earth.

(Acts 8.32–33)

Perhaps in reading this passage, the eunuch remembered how he too had been brought, without his consent, before those who would castrate him. Justice had been denied him also. When he died, his life too would be taken from the earth. Maybe he is struck not just by the description of a sacrificial lamb, but by the fact this story resonated with his own experience.

Within the traditional telling of the story the eunuch's inquiry after baptism might be interpreted as something like conversion, or an identification that this is the logical outcome of the conversation. Occasionally it is even seen as symbolizing the effectiveness of Philip's witness. In the context of a silenced victim, perhaps in response to the question 'What is to prevent me being baptized?', he expected Philip to list off the obstacles. Philip's response, and the eunuch's baptism, might contain deeper truth than simply becoming a Christian. In baptism, the eunuch receives a name instead of a label, a future instead of annihilation, and an identity not based on what he lacked.

In this example, recognizing the power of our own spiritual and social culture to skew our interpretation of Scripture unlocks new insight into well-known stories.

Wider culture

Despite the impression Christians often accept, that we live in a 'biblically illiterate' society, there is evidence to the contrary. Judas has appeared in popular music videos, apples represent temptation in many advertisements, Eve is the universally sinful woman. And one of Jesus' parables has been used by almost all the prominent politicians of the last 30 years, from Jeremy Corbyn to Jacob Rees Mogg, Margaret Thatcher to Gordon Brown. The story has been used to support military action, market economics and government spending. All kinds of institutions borrow their title from the hero of the parable. We have Good Samaritan hospitals, schools and even pubs. The UK now has on its statute book a law to protect 'Good Samaritans' from prosecution if their rescue attempts fail. Wider culture has disconnected the parable almost entirely from its biblical roots, remembering only that a man (often with money) rescued somebody who had fallen on hard times.

Returning to the tradition, the biblical text highlights the domestication of the story. First, Jesus does not call the man 'good', although he is very clear that he was a Samaritan. Which means he was not one of the powerful going to rescue one of the weak, but one of the despised rescuing one of the privileged. He was not being good or heroic, in Jesus' story, but a 'neighbour' – something which we all are. The parable has much to say about the privileged needing to accept help from the despised. Returning to tradition enables an exegesis that critiques contemporary attitudes.

What does a four-source model of theological reflection bring to exegesis?

Often in theological training, exegesis has meant uncovering something of what the text originally meant, either in the mind of its author or to the first hearers. The approach achieves critical distance from the text, freeing it, allegedly, from the biases of its interpreter. Reading the text from the source of Tradition in a four-source reflection on the text can include historical-critical methodology, but is not limited to it. Such a reading might begin with the original writers or readers in mind, but move through a range of interpretation developed down through church history, which allows the exegete to ponder commonalities across history and culture, commonalities among the communities into which the text is received.

Historical-critical methods risk focusing on authority and historicity. They might inspire the question 'is this true?' Approaching a text by way of four sources is more likely to raise the question 'is it truthful?' As Karl Barth said:

> I have nothing whatever to say against historical criticism. I recognize it and once more state quite definitely that it is both necessary and justified. My complaint is that recent commentators confine themselves to interpretation of the text which seems to me to be no commentary at all, but merely the first step towards a commentary.
>
> (1968, 6)

Reading from tradition alone, as with any historical-critical method, distances the biblical text so that it can be objectively examined. It does not, however, recover the gap thus created, enabling the text to speak today. It is by exploring the text from the three other perspectives that our view of it becomes more whole.

Once the exegete has arrived at an adequate interpretation from the perspective of tradition, they might choose to interrogate it from a cultural perspective. How, for example, did the text come to mean a particular thing at a particular time? Which aspect of that meaning resonates today? In my chapter on preaching I draw a comparison between two cataclysmic events – the fall of Jerusalem in 70 CE and the attack on the World Trade Center in 2001.

A different cultural perspective vital for exegesis leading to preaching is how a biblical passage might be understood in today's culture. The story is told that a new member was asked to read the Old Testament passage in church one Sunday. Reaching the end of a particularly violent and blood-thirsty text, they turned to the liturgical sentence and intoned '*this* is the word of the Lord?!' Much of what the Bible seems to say sounds anathema to modern ears, but when viewed from the perspective of its own culture appears innocuous. Abraham's amenability to child sacrifice is sometimes seen as a sign of his great faith. If, however, we ask why he seeks no instruction on how to do this, it becomes apparent that it was part of contemporary religious culture – he didn't need to ask, because he knew what to do. Then the story becomes more about God than about Abraham.

It is when we arrive at the other two sources that this method of exegesis comes into its own. Other exegetical methods reveal truths in Scripture. Examining a biblical text from the perspective of Experience and Position add something distinctive to the mix.

First, the admission that we always come to the Bible as ourselves, vision coloured by the experiences that have formed us, both good and less good. This is a point at which some preachers baulk, as I discuss in my chapter on preaching. However, if we believe that God has formed us (Psalm 139) then we might also accept that we have been formed to read this passage out of who we are. Personal experience can be a route to general truth.

Experience that resonates with something in Scripture might bring new insight into old text. I remember a disabled student giving an exegesis of Judges 3.12–30. In it, after 18 years of oppression by the Moabites, God frees Israel through a judge called Ehud. The Bible points out that Ehud was left-handed. Ehud made a double-edged sword and strapped it to his right thigh before he went into the presence of the king. He was able to do this because as a left-handed person he could draw a sword from his right thigh. He was able to get away with it because the king's guards would have checked the left thigh of those visiting the king. Ehud was God's instrument because of his difference. My student was able to speak on this passage from personal experience, with an authenticity unavailable to anyone else in the room. Conversely, experience of being on the 'wrong' side of Scripture might raise important questions too, with potential for new insight.

Acknowledging personal position as we come to a biblical text is essential, too. Firmly held views influence strongly how we feel about a passage, as illustrated above. We may desperately seek a new interpretation because what seems to be the most obvious goes against firmly held beliefs. This can be fruitful in two ways: first, we might find a viable new interpretation; second, we might change our minds! Whichever of these is true, the experience provides valuable, authentic, first-hand material for a sermon. In this instance, text and reader, separated by the critical distance of other methods, are rejoined in a devotional reading.

There are two types of textual interpretation, according to Gadamer (*Wahrheit und Methode*, 1960): *Verstehen* (understanding), and *Verstandigung* (coming to an understanding with someone or something). Using the four sources available in this model of theological reflection enables both aspects, concluding with a full and holistic exegesis.

What about commentaries?

Where do commentaries fit into this method of exegesis? First, let's acknowledge there are risks with commentaries. Just as historical-critical methods of exegesis can distance the text from the reader, so commentaries can distance the reader from the text. Rather than come to it in person we substitute another reader, the one who wrote our commentary.

Bearing that in mind, however, we must accept the value of commentaries. I would simply say that while they are not a primary source for exegesis, they are a very useful secondary one. Each of the four sources might raise a number of questions. Once we have identified which ones are significant enough to need answering, a commentary, or preferably several, is the place to go. Of course, a quick theological reflection on the commentary itself might be needed – who wrote it, what is their culture or tradition, and so on.

Exegetical shape

Having gone through the stages of reflecting theologically on a passage, or passages, of Scripture, a range of material will be at hand. It is unlikely, however, that the finished product should be shaped around the four sources. The outcome of reflection should be integrated to enlighten the text.

What follows is part of a talk I gave at a Women's Voices conference in 2017. I have tried to note in brackets which element of my theological reflection influenced my exegetical decisions. My aim was to present new insights into the character of Mary, the mother of Jesus. You will notice that I have used P (Position) whenever I have included a personal interpretation of the text, rather than only for the expression of my own views.

Mary: revolutionary and resilient

If you were asked to list the main issues that divide the Protestant Church from the Roman Catholic, I wonder what you would say? I imagine that near the top would be the role of women. Possibly the theology of ordination. Just over 20 years ago, when answering the same question, Pope John Paul II gave as one of his top five contenders the person of Mary. (T)

That probably sounds strange to us. We don't really 'do' Mary. Where, in Catholic countries, Mary is ever present in one form or another, for us she fades in and out. Despite her necessary presence at the birth of the Son of God, Mary seems to function largely as wallpaper, made necessary in the story because God had decided to be born. Of the small number of Christmas carols that mention her (only 3 of the top 10), other than the fact that she had a womb, we learn only that she was a 'mother mild', serene in 'maiden bliss'. (C)

That is not, I want to contend, the Mary of the Bible. The Gospel writers' portrayal is far from the pale insipid characterization we see in much artwork.

Let's go in search of the missing Mary of the Bible.

Matthew and Luke both give Mary a context that is easily missed. (T) She has a context in the history of God's people. Mary is the Westernized version of her name – she would have been Miriam to her contemporaries, Miriam of Nazareth still, in Jewish and Muslim literature. And Miriam is a name freighted with meaning for the Jewish people. Miriam was Moses' older sister, the woman who helped rescue Moses, who ensured that Pharaoh's daughter hired his, and her, own mother as his nurse; the one who accompanied Moses when he led the people of Israel out of captivity; the one who helped declare freedom to the people of God. Mary has a name that speaks of God's mighty deeds, of scattering the proud, the humbling of rulers and sending away the rich; a name synonymous with mercy, with lifting up the humble and filling the hungry with good things.

Matthew similarly gives Mary a context in the narrative of God's people. He tags her on to his begettings and begattings, at the end of his genealogy. A closer look shows that while Abraham may have begotten Isaac, who begat Jacob, by verse 3 Tamar comes into the story; and after a few more 'fathers of' we have Rahab, almost immediately followed by Ruth and then Bathsheba. There's a long patriarchal list, reflective of the status quo, punctuated by women. I've been around the Church all my life, and yet in the rare sermon I have heard on Matthew's genealogy the best explanation for these women being included is that God is gracious, or perhaps God was making a point by including sinners and foreigners in the list. (E)

I want to suggest there is more to it than that. (P) Tamar married a son of Judah. In those days women were dependent on men – father, husband or son. Tamar's husband, Judah's son, died. Her brother-in-law should have given her a child but because the child would not be his, he practised coitus interruptus. She is cheated out of her child. Judah takes her into his house and keeps her as a single woman. Seeking justice, Tamar pretends to be a prostitute and when her father-in-law goes looking for sex she is there. He cannot pay straight away so leaves the equivalent of his credit card (C) with her until he can arrange payment. When she becomes pregnant he condemns her, so she whips out the credit card and reveals who the father is. It could almost be the stuff of soap operas. Tamar disrupts the prevailing power structures by claiming justice for herself. (T)

Then there's Rahab, commonly known as Rahab the Harlot. The story goes that Joshua, a once highly successful spy and now leader of the Israelites, selects his two best spies to go into Jericho on a highly secret mission. They are immediately discovered, and have to depend on the prostitute Rahab to get them to safety in return for a promise that she too will be safe. This is the stuff of comedy, incompetent men rescued by a lowly woman. (T)

And Ruth, who is loyal to her mother-in-law and the God of Israel and through some well-planned shenanigans in the harvesting barn, persuades Boaz to marry her. And Bathsheba, spotted by the king while carrying out her religious duties, subsequently raped by him but ultimately a queen. (T)

These four have more in common than just incongruous inclusions in Matthew's genealogy. Each of them in her own way confronts injustice, exposes inequality and ensures a future for the underdog. Then says Matthew, there was Joseph, 'the husband of Mary, and Mary was the mother of Jesus' (Matthew 1.16). Mary is introduced in the context of courageous women who have challenged and changed things.

I want to suggest that far from being meek and mild, a convenient incubator for the Son of God, Mary is revolutionary and resilient, an inconvenience for most of the Church. Tradition may have rendered her mild and almost invisible, but I don't think the Gospels do. (P)

Let's start with Luke. If Luke had written his Gospel the way the Church often reads it, there would be an ethereal submissive girl, chosen for her compliance, agreeing to have a baby for God. She would then disappear. We might, by chance, come to realize that this same woman uttered the oldest Christian hymn we have. It is certainly the most passionate, the wildest, the most revolutionary hymn ever sung. This is not a gentle, tender dreamy Mary. Not the Mary we often see in paintings or sculptures. There is no nostalgia, none of the sweetness of 'Away in a manger', none of the encouragement to eat, drink and be merry that we find in 'God rest ye merry gentlemen' ... presumably while the gentlewomen get the cooking and the washing-up done. No meek mild baby lying in a manger here. (C)

This is a hard, strong, powerful song about God, God's reign in the world, and the powerlessness of humankind to stop it.

Mary is inspired to sing the song when she meets her cousin Elizabeth, the barren woman now pregnant. It is Elizabeth's prophetic recognition of Mary that prompts her to break into song. I wonder how often we affirm others and release them into a greater ministry than our own. (T)

Mary is usually portrayed as singing this sweetly, in meek acceptance of her faith, and maybe her fate. (T) But I wonder what really strikes her when she arrives at her cousin's house. Here is Elizabeth, who has longed for a child for many years. Here is her home, ready for the baby, in a mood of celebration despite Zechariah's strange silence. Here is joy at the prospect ahead, and as Mary arrives the baby is quickened too – there really is life inside Elizabeth. (E)

For Mary the story is different. Pregnancy outside marriage was not uncommon in those days, Roman soldiers regularly and impunitively raped the girls of the countries they invaded – a custom as much of modern armies as of the Roman army back then. But in a culture not that different from our own, if a girl was raped and became pregnant it was deemed to be her fault. So, despite the sacred provenance of Mary's child, she would be shamed for her pregnancy. She faced a life marred by the gossip of her neighbours, the suspicion of her friends, and the lack of security implicit in the lack of a husband. (C)

Arriving at Elizabeth's Mary knew two things at one and the same time – she faced a difficult time ahead – and this baby was from God. And so, I suspect (P) that the Magnificat was a song of defiance, a song of acknowledgement that God was in control, that she would submit to her task, but that it might involve significant personal cost.

Mary's song is a song of praise from the midst of suffering and conflict. A defiant song of worship about a radically intervening God, from somebody living in mental and social torment. (P)

And as a result, the Magnificat is perhaps best understood by those who identify with Mary's position at the time. The oppressed. Frequently throughout history the marginalized have been inspired and encouraged by the words of this poem. Inspired to believe that God sees their plight and encouraged to think that he might do something about it. (C)

Interestingly, it has also been oppressors who have understood the deep meanings of the Magnificat. In the 1980s the government of Guatemala banned the song, suspecting that its preference for the poor might stir a revolution. The mothers of the disappeared in Argentina put the words of the Magnificat on their posters when they protested, and the military junta of Argentina banned those words from being put on show. Perhaps most shamefully of all during the occupation of India, the British also banned the Magnificat that was sung each Sunday in churches back home. (C)

Mary was prophesying a new reign of God, a commonwealth in which there was no exploitation, no oppression, no dehumanization. And she did it from the experience of exactly that. She did it with joy – and through gritted teeth.

Sometime later, the son of this woman who declared God's overthrowing of the powerful, dismissing of the rich and blessing of the lowly, proclaimed that he had come to bring good news to the poor, release to the captives, sight to the blind and freedom to the oppressed (T). Jesus was his mother's son. Mary does not disappear, she is not merely a conduit through whom God is incarnated – she is the mother of Jesus, and he carries some of her characteristics. The wonder of the incarnation is not that God passed through the body of Mary, but that

God took on human personality as well as divine in order to embody the covenant between humanity and divinity. (T/P)

You know well the story of a woman confronting Jesus and telling him he was wrong. I have marked several assignments on it, one of which suggested that Jesus simply had the first-century equivalent of a bad pizza the night before and was feeling rough, so the woman told him to behave. (E) When I mention a woman confronting Jesus most of you I guess will think of the Syro-Phoenician woman, and think about how hard it is to explain. (C) But what about Luke 2? As a 12-year-old lad, Jesus takes it on himself to stay in the big city rather than go home with his family. And he doesn't bother to tell them. They travelled for a day before they realized he was missing, they travelled another one before they found him. He was sitting calmly chatting with the teachers, who were amazed at his wisdom. But his parents were astonished. (T) I bet they were! Astonished at his knowledge, or at his lack of thought, is not clear. Mary ticks him off. Now because Luke goes on to tell us that Jesus calls the Temple his Father's house and suggests that his parents should have known he would be there, and because they don't under-stand, we tend to take Jesus' perspective in this. He was right, and they were dozy. (P) But could it just be that actually Mary was giving him an early lesson in how to treat other people? If Jesus was truly human, he needed to learn human skills from somewhere. He did, after all, go home and obey his parents and grow in wisdom after this incident.

If that isn't confrontational enough for you, what about the wedding at Cana in John's Gospel? They run out of wine, Mary notices. She goes to Jesus who tells her it isn't any of her business and he isn't ready to do anything about it. Surely a meek and mild Mary would have butted out at that point. Not the Mary of John's Gospel, though. She overrides him, tells the servants to do whatever he tells them (T), and then – in my head at least – turns to Jesus with a look that says, 'Come on then, now's the time to start.' (P) And Jesus launches his ministry, in a very homely setting, at the bidding of his mother.

Mary is inconvenient, because when we really get to know her, she doesn't leave room for us, the women disciples who come after her, to be meek, mild, compliant or any of the other characteristics tradition might entreat us to develop.

I don't have time now to think about Mary's presence at the cross or in the upper room awaiting the day of Pentecost – read it for yourselves. But let me leave Mary with this thought: Perhaps if we really get to know Mary all generations might eventually call her blessed.

7

Reflective preaching

LIZ SHERCLIFF

Introduction

In this chapter I will explore my personal use of theological reflection in preaching. My practice has grown out of the four-source model (Experience, Position, Culture, Tradition). As I explore the sources, I include some samples from sermons to which theological reflection led. I do so because I hope that they will be helpful and illustrative, not because of their particular excellence.

Elsewhere, I have defined preaching as

> ... the art of engaging the people of God in their shared narrative by creatively and hospitably inviting them into an exploration of biblical text, by means of which, corporately and individually, they might encounter the divine.[1]

Implicit are three voices that are not only key to the sermon, but also participants in preparatory reflection. The first is the preacher, the one engaging and inviting; the second is the congregation, those being invited individually and corporately to explore and encounter; the third is the biblical text, the locus of this exploration.

This reflective model differs distinctly from patterns of preaching typified in the early 1960s by Jean-Jacques von Allmen: 'God is not so much the object as the true source of Christian preaching. Preaching is thus speech *by* God rather than speech *about* God' (1962, 7). An image of this kind of preaching might be an arrow, symbolizing a message from God through the preacher to a passive congregation. In the world of this image the preacher occupies a powerful position, frequently described as 'six feet above criticism'. The community brings no knowledge of its own, and simply receives. God does not appear in the image but is, rather, above it, the supreme being firing the penetrating arrow through the preacher and beyond.

In postmodern times, a model of preaching dependent on assumed authority seems foreign to the culture. Postmodernity brings with it heightened self-awareness, which expects consultation rather than instruction. Preachers, then, need to begin with their own 'situated-ness'.

Adult learning

Having been involved in adult education for the past 30 years I confess to giving an indulgent smile when newly selected ministry trainees share their beliefs about preaching. Among certain branches of the Church at least, there happily roost those who believe that the task of the preacher is to tell the congregation what the Bible/God says. If they do it well enough, people will not only hear, but amend their ways accordingly. Early conviction contrasts sharply with later lament that congregations appear not to change, despite passionate pronouncements made by their clergy. Even in church it remains the case that people do not learn simply because they are told.

Exegesis

Many a lecture, or textbook, or even assignment brief in the area of homiletics expounds the virtue of an exegesis–application sermon model. Work out the key themes of the text then apply them to life. Churches have been using the model for decades, and there is scant evidence of its efficacy. A significant problem is its basis in an assumed presupposition-less interpretation, ignoring the fact that every reader of the Bible comes to it with their own experiences of life and faith, and their own fundamental beliefs. Even as the preacher seeks wisdom from the text their search is swayed by conscious and unconscious convictions. Application is problematic too. Without real reflection, the sermon easily descends into the premise that 'we all'. The linear structure of an exegesis–application structure is restrictive, rather than expansive, often basing its rationale on norms embraced by the speaker, but not necessarily shared by hearers.

A few years ago, I was invited to write an article exploring whether women preach with a different voice (Shercliff, 2014). During the preparatory research I spoke with a large number of Anglican ordinands, most of whom I had actually taught (though, at that time, not in homiletics). The words of one remain my inspiration: 'I feel I have been taught to preach like someone else.' The question left me with a different one: how might we teach preaching? Bringing the preacher overtly into the sermon is part of my answer to that question.

Preaching as 'me'

As the mother whale said to the baby whale, 'You need to be careful. It's when you are spouting you are most in danger of being harpooned.' Preaching can seem a bit like that. It's when we take courage in both hands and stand before a congregation, praying to say something that might enable an encounter with the living God, that we are most in danger of getting it wrong.

No wonder some preachers like to hold God accountable for their words – sometimes justified by apparently sound doctrine: 'The gospel can be seen as a quite definite injunction not to be ourselves' (Moore, 2013, 19); Christ speaks through his messengers; our task is simply to be a conduit; God will use our words no matter how badly formed ... There are doubtless occasions on which God does speak through preachers. Sadly, there are also occasions when preachers make insufficient effort, and blame God for the result.

Occasionally, self-awareness is unwelcome. Perceiving a need to project absolute faith, doubt is suppressed. Rather than admit ourselves to be like Shakespeare's Richard II, 'in one person many people' and possibly 'none contented', we don one of the acceptable masks stored in each vestry cupboard. From the pulpit beams out, we hope, exactly the kind of preacher the congregation hopes to hear from. Meanwhile, our unwanted tendencies are hidden in what Jung called our shadow side. Unfortunately, the less light the shadow side is given, the stronger it grows; the more conscious we become that the faithful, confident preacher we project is a sham, the more we feed it, until eventually it breaks out, and there is no containing it. Working with the shadow self, on the other hand, can be creative, offering insights into faith unavailable elsewhere.

At a recent symposium for preachers we were asked to discuss whether appearance made any difference to the way a sermon is heard. Unsurprisingly, the room was divided. Generally, it was men who deemed it irrelevant. The experience of women among others is different. I have been told, 'I didn't listen to you at first because you're a woman', and 'You were so good, I forgot you were a woman'. Other research reports comments to women preachers that include 'too much or too little make-up, too long or too short hair; too colourful or too dull dress; too low or too high shoes; too long or too shiny earrings; or too long or too red fingernails' (Brown, 2003, 13). Rather than reveal feminine curves, many women prefer to hide behind shapeless clothing or androgynous robes (Copeland, 2014).

Congregations have expectations of their preachers, based on what they first see – robes, chinos, earrings all convey meaning as the preacher stands to speak. And what do we say of the differently abled, or those from ethnic minority groups? Assumptions and prejudices spring unbidden and unnamed to the congregational mind before the preacher utters their opening sentence. It simply will not do to say that the preacher is merely an invisible conduit for the sermon. Congregations notice age, gender and ethnicity, and allocate different regard to each.

In addition to God and the false self, commentaries offer another excellent hiding place for preachers. There are excellent commentaries, made use of by students and preachers alike. 'Commentary work' forms part of much teaching on ordination courses. There are even commentaries written on the assumption that ministers are too busy to prepare thoroughly to preach. In the model of preaching I have offered, this is of course inadequate. As well as inviting hearers into a space defined by a biblical text, the preacher is 'called to be a *witness*, one who sees before speaking, one whose right to speak has been created by what has been seen' (Long, 1988, 4).

Whether we hide theologically behind God, physically behind shapeless clothes, psychologically behind masks, or academically behind commentaries, one fact remains: when we preach we *are* seen. We stand as embodied people before the congregation. Whether we like it or not, before we open our mouths, they have formed opinions about us and ascribed value to what we have not yet said.

So, preachers need to do what might be called 'ego work'. Who am I? What makes me respond to certain things in certain ways? What in me is of God, and what is not? Lack of such reflection leads easily to inauthenticity. I take comfort from the words of Barbara Brown Taylor:

> I have learned things in the dark that I could never have learned in the light, things that have saved my life over and over again, so that there is really only one logical conclusion. I need darkness as much as I need light. We do need dark times, but we also need friends like Martha to call us out of them. Once Martha has realized that Jesus is the Christ, she goes to tell her sister 'Jesus has come for you too.'
>
> (2014, 5)

Self-awareness, acceptance of what is dark in our experience or position, is the quintessence of authentic preaching. Some time ago I was given a reading on which my sermon was to be based, and a title to work to. The reading was Psalm 91, and the title 'Dealing with Doubt'. A few months earlier my daughter had been seriously ill. As she lay in the Intensive Care Unit, expecting to die, I was advised to read this psalm to her. I had found it unhelpfully triumphalistic. The experience raised questions about the psalm, and about certainty. In preparing to preach, this experience and the questions to which it gave rise were at the forefront of my mind. I decided that rather than hide behind a mask of sure faith, I would be honest. Here is part of the introduction to my sermon that day:

> I don't know how you felt hearing the readings for today. As I looked at them and looked at the brief for today's sermon, I suspected I was supposed to say that as Christians we don't need to fear or be anxious about anything.
>
> I'm not sure I can say that.
>
> I have to admit that I am a bit allergic to the psalm we had read. When our daughter was lying very ill in intensive care somebody recommended that I read it to her. She and I both found it profoundly unhelpful – here we were being encouraged to believe that we would not fear the terror of the night, that we need not fear pestilence and that God would give his people long life, when it was acutely plain that that coming night would be very testing, that the pestilence was rendering my daughter's body helpless and that not only might life not be long but that it was possibly not going to outlast the week.
>
> So what can we say about fear and anxiety?

Key to 'the art of engaging the people of God' and 'inviting them into an exploration of biblical text' is not the ability to satisfactorily complete a weekly task of sermon preparation. It is to lead a preaching life (Taylor, 2013), one of continuous reflective ego work.

Inviting the congregation

Implicit in my definition of preaching is the role of preacher as 'host', the one who invites the congregation, individually and corporately, to explore and encounter. As host we need to know something about our invitees.

'Relevance' is a widely accepted standard for good preaching often questioned by new preachers. Congregations are diverse, with different needs and expectations. It is not possible to preach relevantly to all, and we should abandon the attempt.

Fortunately, we are called not only to preach to individuals but to congregations, communities of people who form their own culture. Reflecting on congregational culture is as important as knowing ourselves as the preacher called to them. The image for reflection lies before us at the start of every service. What might the building layout say? Are people ready for worship before the service begins, or has the introduction been made and the first song part sung before the congregation is in place? Are people welcomed, or welcomed to 'our service'? Where is the focus? Often the unconscious actions betray attitudes close to the collective heart. Preaching unmasks hidden attitudes to the congregation – are they sentient people of God, or an audience for the preacher? Do they contribute, or are they told?

I was invited to preach at a small church just after their honorary part-time minister left. The congregation was elderly and probably the majority suffered ill health. The reading was Matthew 14.22–33, Peter walking on the water. The departed minister asked me to talk about Peter's faith and how the Church would survive if only its members would dare to walk on water. Reflecting on the congregation prompted me to what I think was a more realistic approach. These people had, I knew, given years of faithful service to the Church. Many had joined this daughter church from the main parish because they found the band-led worship too loud and the screen-dominated liturgy difficult to read. There was already a sense of rejection among them. Encouraging them to do what they physically could not would only lead to discouragement, I suspected.

I returned to the passage, looking for a way of reading that might speak to a bruised and fearful congregation. This is part of what I said:

Apparently, although Peter has believed that it really was Jesus, and has got out of the boat, and has walked on the water, and has put his trust in Jesus far more than the others who stayed in the boat … Jesus ticks him off. 'You of little faith, why did you doubt?'

Is that really how it happened? Or can we read the story differently?

Could it be that instead of it being Peter who had the faith, it was the others? Wasn't Peter being a bit like the annoying show-off waving his hand in the air and shouting, 'pick me, pick me'? Was it at this point, when Peter wanted to share in the moment with Jesus, that he most went astray? Did he want to leave the place of fear, the boat, and go to a place where he would be admired and comforted?

Surely Jesus might have considered responding with, 'Who do you think you are, Peter? Sit back down and leave this to me.' But he knew that what Peter really needed was a couple of steps on the water to help him realize who Jesus was, and a nosedive into the sea to help him realize who he was.

I think that is a fair reflection of what happens to us in times of fear. Jesus assures us that he is there with us, but we want to be called out of that place into an easier place, a place where there are no anxieties, but where all is calm.

And that is our real time of doubt. It is when we are unable to trust that he is with us in the tough times, and so pray to be taken out of them, that we most demonstrate our lack of faith …

Perhaps rather than being a story about a heroic disciple who was willing to risk his life to demonstrate who Jesus is, this is actually a story about the other eleven, who never thought of themselves as heroes, who never dreamed of putting Jesus to the test, who were willing to keep rowing against the wind until he got into the boat with them no matter how long it took.

They were just looking for their Lord to join them where they were – and that was where the miracle happened. Not out on the water with Peter doing fancy tricks, but in the boat.

It was when Jesus joined them in the boat that the storm ceased.

Congregations, and their preachers, exist in a wider cultural context too. Not just *Coronation Street* or *EastEnders*, a United or City one, but the *zeitgeist*, the way life feels. In Britain, and much of the Western world, the climate seems to be one of turbulent change – post-Brexit, post-Trump, post-church, postmodern. While experts do not agree on the particularities of contemporary culture, observing the way advertisers in particular communicate can be revealing. No longer do they sell products, but stories. Some advertisements leave mention of the product to the very end. People, apparently, like stories. And while GPs and other professionals might bemoan the fact that patients visit having already checked out symptoms and diagnosed conditions on the internet, this might actually betray a quest for truth.

When preachers and writers dismiss postmodernism as anathema to the Christian faith, perhaps in reality they are simply bemoaning their reduced authority.

The postmodern challenge to rationalism does not mean that truth is to be abandoned, but rather that it will be taken 'seriously enough to go back to the drawing board and re-examine what truth can mean' (Knowles, 2011, 9). Narrative need not be dispensed with, but rather returned to. In a culture seeking a better story, the Christian faith offers exactly that.

Following on from the British referendum on Europe I was asked to preach on Matthew 25.31–46. I knew that the congregation was of divided opinion, and most felt uncertain about the future. I did not want to focus on a contentious issue, but had to recognize it as context. The 'oneness' with which people usually gathered felt fractured, so I was concerned to draw them together in this sermon. Preaching the obvious (to some) heaven, hell and final judgement did not sit well with me at the best of times. Rather than closely exegete the passage, I decided to explore its context.

This is part of that sermon:

I was in the office the day it happened. My son had returned from Istanbul the previous day, his flight leaving just before a bomb went off in the city centre. My husband was at home planning a business trip to the Middle East. My daughter was working in Greece.

In my office one person had flicked on to the BBC News website, and her shock rippled around the room. Realization followed later. People gathered around and stared at the screen, nobody wanted to go back to their desks. Silence pervaded. The flapping of a blind near an open window the only sound. The computer had no sound card, and so we watched silently, as equally silently, over and over again, two planes flew into the twin towers of the World Trade Center in New York, and the towers began to fall.

There was no appropriate reaction – nothing like this had happened before. This was not, we already sensed, a major incident. This was a cataclysmic change to the world as we knew it. Things would never be the same again.

And they haven't ever been the same again.

We live in a constant state of fear. Defending ourselves, no matter how, is acceptable. Suspicion of others is an overriding emotion.

Matthew wrote his Gospel to Christians who had gone through something equally cataclysmic.

The Jerusalem Temple had been in place for over a thousand years, allegedly on the very spot where Abraham had built the altar to sacrifice his son Isaac. For centuries, every day before dawn, a priest had shed the blood of a lamb on the high altar, reaffirming the covenant between God and his people. Despite attacks on it over the centuries, the Temple had always survived – this symbol of God's love for his people was rebuilt after the Babylonians destroyed large parts of it; after the Syrians installed statues of their own gods in it; even after an early version of the Olympic Games was held within its precincts. As long as the Temple stood the Jews had hope, and the Jewish followers of Jesus believed that he had come to fulfil the covenant represented by this enormous building.

But in the year 70, Emperor Vespasian decided to erase the hope the Jews found in their Temple once and for all. The events of that day are still unparalleled throughout history. The Roman army deliberately and ruthlessly literally took the Temple apart, so that not one stone was left on top of another. It could not possibly be rebuilt. The altar was smashed into tiny pieces.

The Temple was annihilated.

The world had changed.

How do we invite people into the sermon space? Here I told my personal account of an event the congregation and I almost certainly had in common. I spent time crafting the story because I wanted people to enter the scene, and the sermon, not just hear it. A similar strategy is useful when preaching to unknown congregations. Rather than offer a long introduction I let them know something about myself through the first part of my sermon. Almost everyone is interested in other people, and this makes opening up the sermon space relatively easy. Here is an example:

> A couple of weeks ago I took my nearly two-year-old grandson to Dunham Massey deer park. It all looked very promising. The sun was shining and as we got into the park area a group of deer had already emerged from the woods and children slightly older than Tobyn were hand feeding them leaves and branches. I thought that would entertain him for a while. But it wasn't what Tobyn wanted. He made it clear he wanted to move on.
>
> The thing was, that earlier this year I had taken him there with his two older cousins. And on that occasion the deer had not come out of hiding, but had remained in the trees and difficult to spot. The children had had great fun finding deer among the trees that others simply walked past.
>
> Clearly Tobyn wanted to repeat the experience and so we set off through the park to the remotest end, and then began walking back as quietly as a one-year-old can manage.
>
> Sure enough, though, Tobyn found some deer. And he was very pleased with himself. What was even more striking was that other people walked past, without seeing the deer that we were watching.
>
> It made me think about today's reading.

I prefer to think of sermon crafting rather than sermon writing. I believe care should be taken not just with what we say, but how we say it. Reflection, therefore, is not just for sermon preparation, it is equally important in sermon editing. Re-reading drafts of a sermon highlights where sentences do not flow, and reveals our own responses to what we intend to say. In the sermon on Matthew 25 I went on to say:

> Fear pervaded everything. Christians and Jews betrayed each other to the Roman authorities, for the sake of their own survival. Faith became private so that people had no evidence on which to base an accusation. Strangers became objects of suspicion. Foreigners were to be feared. Resources were to be kept for ourselves first – charity begins at home.
>
> This was the world and the church to which Matthew wrote his Gospel. In this climate of fear and distrust one of the biggest issues faced by Christians was this: how should we live as followers of Jesus in a world that has turned against us, where we live in fear of others, where self-preservation is the top priority?

And in his response, Matthew includes this story.

Writing not to people in power but often to those who were power-less, Matthew talks about the importance of the nations showing compassion to those in need, the poor, the hungry, the ill-treated.

This is what you do when things are going against you, he says: 'Show mercy.' And in this passage about the judgement of the nations, surely the message is also 'work for your nation to show mercy'.

I tried to phrase a question Matthew's readers might have asked in a way that resonated with my hearers: 'How should we live as followers of Jesus in a world that has turned against us, where we live in fear of others, where self-preservation is the top priority?' It was also intended to infer the post-Brexit climate. I sought to give an answer without directly telling people how to behave. Matthew told his church: 'Show mercy'. The structure was intended to communicate directly and, I hoped, to be memorable.

There is a viable alternative to relevance, I suggest. As I said earlier, relevance demands some kind of equivalence between what is said and hearers' experiences. A 'relevant' can be something like a spider's web. By linking the centre links to points around it the structure is maintained. However, the structure is weakened by inappropriate connections, or lack of pertinence. When even one thread fails the structure begins to fold. I propose resonance as a powerful alternative. A sermon crafted with solicitude can be like a stone dropped into a still pond. It causes ripples that reach every part.

John Chrysostom, one of the Early Church Fathers, said Scripture should not be read as an instruction book, or a source of meaning from which truth must be mined. We should read it, he said, as a letter from a friend and read the love between the lines. When the preacher reads that love and invites others into it, the sermon resonates.

Exploring the biblical text

When faced with a biblical passage, some preachers will, with surprising regularity, reach first for a commentary. Being aware of the importance of context does not necessarily stretch to the immediate context – the text in the hands of the preacher. Yet it is into the text, not the commentary, that the preacher will ultimately invite their hearers. Such an invitation requires knowledge not about the text, but of it. Not the listing of facts type of knowledge, but knowledge that enables us to show others around. 'Knowledge about' gives an impression of authority, the sage on the stage; knowing demonstrates comfortable familiarity. Being comfortable with a text enables discussion of its difficulties, even in the absence of resolution. In the sermon quoted above, I worked to neither dismiss nor over-explain the psalm. I described myself as 'allergic' in the hope this would convey discomfort and acceptance of it.

At the heart of reflective preaching is, I think, approaching the congregation with respect, recognizing that they too have experiences of life and of God, and that God not only might speak to them, but already has. Such respect requires mutuality. The right to speak about the struggles of others is earned through honesty and vulnerability, allowing others to see where the Bible challenges us.

Exegesis is helpful in many ways, but it cannot ultimately do what is the most important. It cannot tell us what this text has to say to this congregation on this occasion: 'The preacher, not the commentator, is the one sent by these people at this moment to this text, and, therefore, only the preacher truly knows the full range of questions to ask' (Long, 2016). However tempting the commentary might be, its writer has never been sent by your congregation to that text at that time. The writers can only answer their own questions. The responsibility of the preacher is to ask of the text first their own questions and then those of their congregation.

Approaching our text for the first time, aware, through theological reflection, of ourselves and our congregations, the third piece of the sermon lies before us – the Bible. An image can be helpful. Is the Bible a letter from God, an instruction manual, a book of wisdom? Our image will determine how we handle Scripture and what we might expect. Effectively we will be working in the world of our image. What is this world like? If our image of the Bible is anything like Van Gogh's still life painting, we might expect light to come from its pages.

Turning to a specific passage we might begin a reflection by asking what the world of the passage is like. Unlike historical-critical methods of criticism, the question opens a wide range of responses, for the world of the text is both its original context and its contemporary one. Some of the sources from a more traditional method of theological reflection are useful – what is my experience of the text? What is my position on it? How do its key themes relate to issues in contemporary culture? How has it traditionally been used? Could it be interpreted differently?

Some time ago I was invited as guest speaker to a large church. I knew very little about the congregation, but was very familiar with the text, Mark 9.35, 37: 'Whoever wants to be first must be last of all and servant of all ... Whoever welcomes one such child in my name welcomes me, and whoever welcomes me welcomes not me but the one who sent me.' The thing is, I cringe that the contemporary Church's concern for children is apparently accompanied by an equal and coincident disdain for the elderly, so I could not with authenticity raise children up as the hope of the Church, as I had heard others do. I also questioned the logic of the 'first shall be last and the last first' phrase. It seemed not to offer a different system, but the same one with different people in power.

Avoiding commentaries, I read and re-read the passage, asking in particular, since I did not know the congregation, 'Where is there good news?' If good news was for the poor only, and they were to become the powerful, then when might they, newly powerful, become those who needed to be made last? Finally, verse 36 began to stand out: 'Then he took a little child and put it among them; and taking it in his arms...' What was the status of children in those days, in Palestine? Where did Jesus get this child from? Had I experience of marginalization that might open up this story? In the example above, I relate this experience to that of being ignored with my grandson as we spotted deer.

At other times, the wider context of the reading might be important. As part of a sermon series on Christian living I was given the passage Ephesians 4.17–32 and the title 'Do Not Grieve the Holy Spirit'. Conversations with members of the congregation had made me aware of disagreement over particular issues. I also knew that the Church genuinely ought to be open to the wider community. For several years preaching had been based on sermon series such as the one in question, meaning that most of the congregation had poor biblical knowledge. I guessed from the theological context that what was expected would be some instructions about how to live. For this sermon I engaged with a considerable amount of commentary work, particularly relating to the structure of the letter and its overall message. I decided to put the verses given into the wider context of the letter to the Ephesians and then hone in on the topic I had been given. Despite the uncertain authorship of the Epistle, which I mentioned in my introduction, I decided to speak as though it were Paul, because that is a possibility, and raising too many doubts was more likely to be unhelpful than not. I wanted to address the issue of unity non-threateningly, but with appropriate challenge.

This is a section from the middle of the sermon:

Let's start at the beginning – Ephesians 1.10 – God's plan in Christ was to gather all things in heaven and earth in him. God's eternal plan is to bring together everything in heaven and on earth into unity. The whole of creation is united in Christ on earth. Unfortunately, what human beings have done is kick God upstairs out of sight so that we don't have to take too seriously the concept of oneness. But oneness, unity, in this case between heaven and earth, is an essential part of the theology of Ephesians.

The theme continues in Ephesians 2.10 'we are what he has made us, created in Christ Jesus for good works, which God prepared beforehand to be our way of life'. Just as humankind has reduced the eternal plan of God to a migration from earth to heaven, and kept God out of the way on earth, so the idea of being created in Christ for good works has been reduced to a kind of morality about which folk can hold ethical discussions – 'do this' but 'don't do that'. But that isn't anything like what Paul says here. What he says is, 'You are God's poem, God's innovation.' Each of us is made uniquely, a poem of God, to do what only we can do on this earth. We are each called to be who only we can be – to play our own full part in the body of Christ. Unity, oneness, is now applied to the relationship between God and God's creatures. We are empowered by the Spirit of God to live out who we were meant to be.

Then, when we each play our part, 'through the church the wisdom of God in its rich variety might now be made known to the rulers and authorities in the heavenly places' (Ephesians 3.10). The existence of unity shows where Jesus is Lord, and nobody else is. God's plan is that radical unity should confound the principalities and powers of this present age. What more powerful message could there be than that for our nation at this time?

So, Ephesians 1.10, heaven and earth will be in unity; 2.10, we are each God's poem designed to be who only we can be, united in the body of Christ; 3.10, unity establishes the kingdom of God on earth. In order to establish this revolutionary unity we are to challenge lies and seek out truth (4.15); we are to live in the power of the resurrection (5.14); and in order to do so we should put on the armour of God (6.13).

Our passage for this morning flows from an earlier verse: 4.15 'But speaking the truth in love we must grow up in every way into him who is the head, into Christ ...'

Paul makes this radical unity – unity of the whole of creation, unity between God and God's creatures, and unity among human beings – the basis of his theology. Speaking the truth in love means working out how this affects what we do and say.

And now we're ready to think about the phrase we have been given this morning – do not grieve the Holy Spirit.

We have been marked with the Holy Spirit of God, as signs and symbols of this unity that is the mark and substance of the reign of God. If that is true then the way we live and speak and relate should be a sign of the redemption of the unity of all things – heaven and earth, the person we are and the person we have been made to be, the kingdom of God and the world in which we live.

Anything that causes disunity grieves the Spirit. That means that God is involved in every aspect of life, every aspect. Christian behaviour is not about keeping some kind of moral code – not doing this or that. It is about living in harmony with God through the power of the Spirit.

Whenever we do something that divides us from another we grieve the Spirit. Whenever we live as though God is not involved in the world, we grieve the Spirit. Whenever we think of ourselves as less than God's unique creation, we grieve the Spirit.

It's the little things that divide – the neighbour who parks a bit inconveniently becomes the idiot who shouldn't be allowed a car; the politician who stands for something we disagree with becomes the potential tyrant who should be run out of office; the earth is important and should be cared for, but I do need an extra carrier bag from the supermarket; those Christians over there don't do things the way I like them, so they are wrong – in fact, they are probably dangerous and I should speak against them. Me? I'm just a housewife, or mother. When we phone somebody, 'Hello, it's just me.' That grieves the Holy Spirit too.

Conclusion

I have sought, in this chapter, to illustrate from my own preaching how theological reflection opens up possibilities for preaching by recognizing the parts of preacher, congregation and Bible in the sermon. These three voices, brought into conversation, inform and guide the mind of the preacher in ways that are not available to the traditional exegesis–application model. The challenge of this practice is the acknowledgement of the preacher as more than a conduit.

Preaching inspired by the four-source model of theological reflection is comfortable in handling sources, almost to the point of making it characteristic of such an approach: it takes seriously the experience of both preacher and congregation (Experience); it gives Scripture enormous respect, like when reading 'a letter from a friend' (Tradition); it grants the preacher permission to hold a strong personal opinion even when possibly viewed as in conflict with Scripture (Position); and it recognizes the situatedness of both preacher and congregation, the air we breathe (Culture).

It renders preaching a bigger task than sermon preparation and requires that we develop the habit of leading a preaching life (Taylor, 2013).

Note

1 'Toward a new homiletic', *Journal of Feminist Theology*, to be published 2018.

8

Using group theological reflection to prepare sermons

LIZ SHERCLIFF

Introduction

In this chapter we look at how theological reflection was used with two groups of students. Based on the outcomes a member of each group (the tutors) prepared and preached a sermon on the same Sunday. The sermons were then given to students for comparison.

The teaching class was made up of 16 recently licensed Readers, led by two tutors. All were conversant with the four-source model of theological reflection.

In preparation for the session, Robin Pye, one of the tutors, read the lectionary reading for a couple of Sundays' time. It was a Sunday in Advent, and the reading was Matthew 11.2–11:

> When John heard in prison what the Messiah was doing, he sent word by his disciples and said to him, 'Are you the one who is to come, or are we to wait for another?' Jesus answered them, 'Go and tell John what you hear and see: the blind receive their sight, the lame walk, the lepers are cleansed, the deaf hear, the dead are raised, and the poor have good news brought to them. And blessed is anyone who takes no offence at me.'
>
> As they went away, Jesus began to speak to the crowds about John: 'What did you go out into the wilderness to look at? A reed shaken by the wind? What then did you go out to see? Someone dressed in soft robes? Look, those who wear soft robes are in royal palaces. What then did you go out to see? A prophet? Yes, I tell you, and more than a prophet. This is the one about whom it is written,
>
> "See, I am sending my messenger ahead of you,
> who will prepare your way before you."
>
> Truly I tell you, among those born of women no one has arisen greater than John the Baptist; yet the least in the kingdom of heaven is greater than he.'

New Testament example

At the start of the session students were divided into two groups of eight. They were told they would be doing a theological reflection, and were given the starting question 'How do you know it's the one?'

Each group did a full reflection, beginning with a thought shower, moving on to key themes, and coming up with an image. The time allowed was well over an hour.

Once the reflection was finished the groups came together and talked each other through their reflections. The Bible passage was then introduced, and a group exegesis carried out.

Tutors photographed each theological reflection and took notes of the exegesis. On the appropriate Sunday each tutor preached a sermon on the same passage in their own churches. These sermons were then shared with the students via the online learning platform.

The theological reflections

Despite starting with the same question, the discussions were very different from each other, often guided by an experience of one or more group members. Experience played a large part in both groups. The question seemed to prompt students to start in that quadrant. In one group the experience related by one student was so striking that they moved naturally to Position. The other group discussed where to go next, and in fact their reflections were scattered among the remaining quadrants.

In answer to the question 'How do you know it's the one?' the first group decided on an image of a well-fitting glove. Key themes explored on the basis of this were belonging, being filled (with the Spirit), coming to life, inhabiting. In group two, the image was of a tick list. This had been prompted by the story one student told of how they had chosen their marriage partner, and in fact how they still make decisions. This image facilitated discussions of how students knew they were right for Reader ministry, or how in Christian tradition the Church has decided on doctrine.

Exegesis

When the larger group came to the biblical passage, their exegesis was heavily influenced by the images as well as the insights they had gained from the theological reflection. It was a rich, multifaceted interpretation of this story from the life of John the Baptist. One group clearly related their tick-box reflection to the kind of Messiah John might have been looking for. The other reflected on a more mutual relationship between

Jesus and John, based on the 'fitting like a glove' image. The sermons too were influenced more by the group reflection than by the class exegesis.

An Old Testament example

This time the student group was less experienced. They had been training for Reader ministry for less than six months and had started Old Testament study two weeks before. The aim of the module was to produce competent preachers, rather than Old Testament scholars, and therefore exegesis and preaching ideas were part of every session.

For this exercise the class had about half an hour.

The text was Amos 5.18–24:

> Alas for you who desire the day of the Lord!
>> Why do you want the day of the Lord?
> It is darkness, not light;
>> as if someone fled from a lion,
>> and was met by a bear;
> or went into the house and rested a hand against the wall,
>> and was bitten by a snake.
> Is not the day of the Lord darkness, not light,
>> and gloom with no brightness in it?
> I hate, I despise your festivals,
>> and I take no delight in your solemn assemblies.
> Even though you offer me your burnt offerings and grain offerings,
>> I will not accept them;
> and the offerings of well-being of your fatted animals
>> I will not look upon.
> Take away from me the noise of your songs;
>> I will not listen to the melody of your harps.
> But let justice roll down like waters,
>> and righteousness like an ever-flowing stream.

An image of a foot trampling a daisy was proposed and agreed. Given time constraints the group decided to work simply with the Culture approach to the image. Rather than report all aspects of the discussion here, I will simply give an indication of how the reflection flowed, and the kind of topics that might have been included in sermons.

Exploring the world of the image, students pointed out that the foot was probably unaware of the damage it was doing; could not avoid doing it; the world is 'just like that'. The daisy could not defend itself, and would be trampled many times a day. The world of the image could be redeemed if the foot were more aware.

Relating the reflection to the passage, students quickly began to explore issues of power in contemporary society, including political, economic and social. Amos' call for justice and righteousness were quickly interpreted in terms of the powerful becoming more aware of the effects of their actions – including powerful Western consumers.

Sermons for Advent

Robin had been in the 'checklist' group. This is his sermon:

> John the Baptist sent his disciples to ask Jesus a question. Actually, he sent them to ask *the* question. Art thou he that should come, or do we look for another? In other words, are you 'the one'?
>
> It is the question that we also ask. It is our faith that the answer to this question is 'Yes'. Christians trust that Jesus is the one that came and is to come – we do not look for another.
>
> John the Baptist sent his disciples to ask the question that we also ask. Which is odd in a way because earlier in Matthew's Gospel, when Jesus comes to be baptized by him, he recognizes Jesus for who he is when he says 'I have need to be baptized of thee, and comest thou to me?'
>
> So he had already recognized Jesus as the one. But he sent his disciples to ask. Was he lying alone in his prison cell and having doubts? Or was he sending his disciples to ask the question so that they would hear the answer from Jesus' own lips?
>
> Either way, Jesus gave an answer that was recorded by the Gospel writer and thus passed down to us so that we might know why he is the one – the real deal.
>
> Or does Jesus give two answers?
>
> Jesus begins his reply to the disciples of John by saying, use your eyes. Use your ears. And then he runs through a checklist. The blind see, the lame walk, the lepers are cleansed, the deaf hear and the dead are raised.
>
> This is a checklist based on the miracles that Jesus has performed that are recorded in Matthew's Gospel. They are also a checklist made up of verses of prophecy from Isaiah.
>
> The blind see. Tick! The lame walk. Tick! The lepers are cleansed. Tick! The deaf hear. Tick! And the dead are raised. Tick! He's ticking all the boxes! And Jesus adds, the good news is proclaimed to the poor – a link to another verse in Isaiah.
>
> Some people need a checklist as a guide to what to do. They use their brains, their logic, their reason. If it all matches up, they make their choice.

Where does this checklist that Jesus uses come from? It comes from Isaiah of course – from the biblical tradition. And through their study of and exposure to Scripture, it would have become hard-wired among many of Jesus' listeners. 'Look, I am the one,' he is saying: 'I tick all the boxes.'

But as well as being a checklist from the tradition, the received wisdom of many of his hearers, Jesus is also running through a checklist that comes from God. After all, Isaiah's prophecies are considered the word of God. And God is our creator. His list of what we want to see in somebody who is 'the one' is hard-wired into all of us. The blind see. The lame walk. The lepers are cleansed. The deaf hear. The dead are raised. Good news is proclaimed to the poor. It's what we want. It's what we need. This is the one. The real deal.

Which is why Jesus throws in an extra catch-all at the end of the checklist. 'And blessed is he, whosoever shall not be offended in me'. Because some people are not using a checklist. They are not feeling an attraction to Jesus because he fulfils the prophecy from Isaiah, although he does fulfil that prophecy.

Some people are just reacting with their heart. Jesus feels like he is the one. The glove fits. It just fits. And they are the blessed. The formality of the checklist falls away. Blessed are they who see the kingdom and run towards it. They can't remember what is on the checklist. They may not even know there is a checklist. They too have eyes. They too have ears. They know what they see and they want to be part of it.

When Jesus runs through the checklist, healing the sick, raising the dead, and proclaiming good news to the poor, he is bringing God's justice into the world. The kingdom of God is at hand.

God's justice contrasts with the judgement of the world. It is the justice we need. It is the blessing of God. Of course the glove fits. Of course it feels right. Of course our checklist points towards it.

But Jesus has to deal now with the fact that John has asked the question, giving expression to doubt.

So Jesus explains that John the Baptist is the real deal. He contrasts John the Baptist with the king who put him in prison, with Herod. Herod is a vacillator – a reed shaken by the wind. Herod lives in a palace and wears soft clothes. In contrast John lives in the wilderness and wears the clothes of a prophet. He never wavers in the wilderness. John lives and speaks like a prophet. You know what a prophet of the kingdom should look like.

If it looks like a duck, walks like a duck and quacks like a duck, it is a duck and the same principle applies to prophets. John the Baptist is the real deal. Jesus says he is the greatest of all the prophets, the greatest man to live – so far.

Which is why Jesus says 'Verily I say unto you, Among them that are born of women there hath not risen a greater than John the Baptist'. But then Jesus adds, 'notwithstanding, he that is least in the kingdom of heaven is greater than he' (meaning greater than John the Baptist).

Jesus is saying that the least of us, we who are all invited into the kingdom of God, we are all greater than John who merely heralded it. John heralded the kingdom but did not live to see it. Trapped in his cell he began to have his doubts because he did not see the kingdom at hand. He had doubts but we should not doubt.

We should not doubt. We are greater than John the Baptist. We can use our eyes. We can use our ears. We can see and hear the things that John the Baptist could not see and could not hear from his prison cell.

How do we know he is the one? Do you use your brain or your heart? Do you use feeling or reason? Science or emotion? You can trust your heart. You can trust your reason. He is the one. He brings the justice of God. He brings the justice you need. You can enter into his kingdom and be a fuller human being than those who came before him. It is the real deal. We trust in him. He is the one. There is no other. Amen.

Liz was in the 'glove' group. This is her sermon:

'Is this the one?'

I guess you, like me, have spent quite a bit of time on that kind of question in recent weeks. 'Is this the one?'

We're encouraged to ask it at this time of year.

In recent weeks I've spent quite a lot of time asking a similar question. 'Is this the one?' I've done my research, I've talked to other people, I've read about it, I've thought about it. It has occupied quite a bit of my time. And yes, I am pretty confident that I have chosen the right Lego for my grandson's Christmas present.

But I won't know – I won't really know – until it comes to Christmas Day and he unwraps it and I see his face. And of course I will know then, because six-year-olds aren't great at hiding their emotions. Last year when he was five I got a little lecture from him on how grandmas shouldn't really buy grandsons pyjamas for Christmas. I will know. But I don't know yet.

In among the glitter and sparkle of Christmas, the joy and celebration, the talk of gifts and God, babies and mothers there is always something unacknowledged. Among the carols and the Christingles, there lurks a question: Is this the one?

Certainty is celebrated. In our television adverts the right gift is chosen and the poor little robin finds its way home to the right mate. Awards are made to sports personalities who were so certain about their abilities, they won. Commentators look back over the year and interpret its events with certainty, despite nobody really understanding what happened.

In church we sing carols and hear sermons and read Bible stories that speak confidently of God coming to earth.

And now we get this very real story about John the Baptist. John the promised baby; John the prophet; John the one who recognized who Jesus was. Or thought he did. He couldn't really know, though. Not yet.

In our reading today we find John asking a hard question. The question.

He had seen the truth, once. He had recognized that Jesus was the one, when he baptized him. But now, from his prison, he couldn't be sure.

So he sent some of his disciples to ask his question. Simple, yet profound:

'Are you the one?'

Are you the one? Or should we expect somebody else?

I wonder what John had been expecting. Maybe he was a bit like my grandson last Christmas, expecting one thing and getting another. Maybe John was expecting a super gift that ticked all the boxes in his head: after all, he had been telling people that someone was coming. Maybe when he looked at Jesus he felt a bit like my grandson when he opened his pyjamas – it wasn't a proper present. This might not be it.

'Are you the one?'

Jesus did not get out his Bible and flip to a text to prove who he was. He did not give a doctrinal treatise about why John should believe. He did not condemn the apparent doubt.

'Am I the one? Go tell John what you hear and see. Tell him what's going on.'

The blind receive sight, the lame walk, those who have leprosy are cleansed, the deaf hear, the dead are raised, and the good news is proclaimed to the poor.

Jesus' response was revolutionary. And it still is.

I've noticed that all too often when somebody asks a Christian whether Jesus really is the one, there's a tendency to revert to argument. To pick up the Bible and spout verses at them; or to choose a famous saying or saint and slap them down before the questioner.

I was invited a while ago to go into a class of sixth formers and talk about why I'm a Christian. Two other Christians from other churches went in as well. One of them started off by saying, 'I became a Christian when I realized that Christ died for my sins.' That's a sentence that makes sense to a lot of us I guess. And the speaker assumed it would make sense to these sixth formers.

There was silence.

And then one brave girl put up her hand and said:

'Who did what for your what?'

She didn't know who Christ was, she didn't understand what the speaker meant by 'dying for me', and she hadn't heard of sin. The sentence was nonsense to her.

And that's the problem when we try to use words to explain the kingdom of God to others. It doesn't make sense.

So Jesus doesn't give good arguments when John's disciples ask whether he is the one. He does something very simple. Go and tell him what you see and what you hear.

What did they see? Liberation. What did they hear? Good news.

Following Jesus was not simply a matter of believing certain things. It was about making a difference and spreading good news.

Jesus' unflinching emphasis, from the start of his ministry to the end, was that he changes things and he is good news.

Would anyone know that Jesus is good news by listening to our conversations? Or watching us do business, or care for our grandchildren, or go about our everyday business?

Jesus didn't send John's disciples back to tell them what they saw Jesus doing. Just what they saw. He didn't tell them to go back and repeat his teaching to John, just that what they heard was good news to the poor.

In Matthew's Gospel Jesus has already sent out the twelve and given them authority. His followers were already doing what he did, and that is what Jesus tells John's disciples to go back and tell John. Jesus isn't telling John about himself, but about the new commonwealth of God in which not only Jesus makes a difference, but his followers do too.

What would happen if churches saw their mission the same way? What would happen if Christians were blessed for what they are doing outside the church instead of feeling we ought to be inside the church more? What if we saw our job as out there, being good news?

Is this the one?

Are we following the Messiah, you and I?

Only if the person we follow inspires and empowers us to make a difference, to be a challenge, to bring good news to the poor. If our Messiah insists simply that we think or say the right things, we are following the wrong one. It isn't the one.

And if our Messiah is the one, if our Messiah makes us good news to the poor, there will be a question for us too:

Are you the one?

The one who will follow despite doubt, who will love radically, rather than cling to dead teaching?

I wonder how John felt when he got this message from Jesus. He is languishing in prison, and he gets to hear of those who are trapped in different ways – by physical illness or disability or by religious rules or by poverty. 'Well, good for them,' he must have thought. 'But I'm still in prison!' It was a message likely to depress rather than lift his spirits.

Except that we can be bound even when we are not ill or disabled or rejected or poor. We can be bound because we see ourselves in that way. Liberation is not a once for all event. How many people were free once, but went back to captivity? For some of us, there is a love of sin, not in the way that we keep on doing something wrong, but because it gives us an excuse. If we continue to regard ourselves as 'just' sinners, we have no responsibility to redeem the world around us. We do not have the challenge that freedom brings with it. But when we see ourselves as truly the forgiven, liberated, righteous people of God then we have to do what Jesus did, just as his disciples had done in the previous chapter of Matthew. Maybe there is a bit in John, as he hears this message, that realizes he too is free, even though he is in prison. He too can bring the kingdom of God to the limited space in which he dwells.

And so what is the Advent message?

Yes, Jesus is the one. He is the one who changes things, who sets us free, one day at a time, so that we too can bring his reign to wherever we are.

Is Jesus the one?

What do you see and hear?

I'd like to pray, if I may:

Spirit of Truth, direct our attention to the life of Jesus, so that we might see what you would have us be. Make us, like him, teachers of your good law. Make us, like him, performers of miraculous cures. Make us, like him, proclaimers of your kingdom. Make us, like him, loving of the poor, the outcast, children. Make us, like him, silent when the world tempts us to respond in the world's terms. Make us, like him, ready to suffer. Amen.

9

Poetry

ANDREW RUDD

A poem is a theological reflection

A poem is a theological reflection. That does not just apply to a religious poem, but any poem. Theology can only originate in human discourse, in the language – there is no other place for it to happen. All the words we use carry an enormous weight of history, world-view, assumptions and ideas about what is real. In the everlasting interplay of human discourse, in speech and writing, cultural norms, values, ideas and expressions are constantly created and renewed.

In all of this a poem is a dedicated space in which language is considered, selected and condensed in a way that is inherently reflective. By its very nature it subjects language to the tension of formal structures. These structures may be complex patterns such as the sonnet, which organize or shape an idea in a way that opens up the possibility of new thinking. They may be strategies as simple as breaking the line, of punctuating the rush of words with tiny pauses for reflection.

Just like any other artist, the poet does not just start out with a set of ideas which are then 'expressed'. The process is much more subtle. Poets set out like Abraham, not knowing where they are going (Hebrews 11.8). And it is in the process of writing itself, that discoveries are made. Some 'religious verse' fails precisely because it begins and ends with a fixed idea, and does not venture anywhere new or unexpected.

Of course, this work of the poem may not be recognized as theological inquiry. Sometimes it may only be when the poem is explicitly placed in a theological context that the reader identifies it as theological – a particular type of 'framing'. Theological exploration in general often begins as a secular, cultural process, coexisting with many other forms of inquiry: only later is it codified and defined as explicitly theological or 'sacred'. David Jasper quotes with approval the suggestion of Stopford Brooke, that in poets 'we see theology, as it were, in the rough; as at its beginnings' (Jasper, 1989, 6).

If we take seriously the claim of Christianity to be an incarnational religion, and if we live in a world 'charged with the grandeur of God'

(Hopkins, 1986, 128), then it is possible to assert that whatever we use to explore and understand experience is necessarily theological. In the words of the Gentile poet quoted approvingly by Paul: 'in him we live and move and have our being' (Acts 17.28).

This is not to suggest that the use of poetry is a requirement of theological reflection in any way, but that poetry – along with all the other forms of art – can be a significant locus of theological reflection.

Poetry and the use of an image in theological reflection

Much of the theological reflection explored in this book makes use of the particular power and affordance of an image. As soon as an image appears in the discussion, it has at least the three following effects:

- It brings the conversation to a single focus.
- It subverts the linear, sequential, 'logical' nature of the discourse.
- It opens the conversation to new possibilities.

Sometimes, when an image appears as part of a conversation in theological reflection, it does not live up to this potential. It can be merely illustrative or diagrammatic, summarizing issues but not taking them anywhere new. The creative process of art – both in its making and its receiving – does something very different. It may be helpful, then, to pay attention to the way in which the discourse of art is different from other discourses, and what this difference offers to theological reflection.

The need to use four sources in itself already supports Mary Midgley's contention that we need to see the world with 'multiple viewpoints'. In her view, 'we peer in at [the world] through a number of small windows ... We can eventually make quite a lot of sense of this habitat if we patiently put together the data from different angles. But if we insist that our own window is the only one worth looking through, we shall not get very far' (Midgley, 2003, 26–7).

It seems necessary to acknowledge that – rich though a four-source model of theological reflection may be – the strand described as Culture has within it many powerful artistic sources and modes of expression. Among many others these include poetry, painting, music and sculpture. Each of these holds the possibility of opening the reflective process to a deeper reality in a way which is unique to that particular modality, a way which cannot be replaced fully by any other. This is not to suggest that theological reflection requires us to engage with every form of human inquiry, every form of art – but, at the very least, it is to encourage an openness to the possibility and excitement that occurs when a 'piece of culture' is attended to, taken seriously, and allowed to speak.

Sustaining joy

That day you surprised me, so full of joy.
Before I could stop myself I said
How will you sustain it? How will
you keep it alive?

But my words
had already pushed your joy
out of the moment.

And of course it didn't last. You talk now
of mountain tops and valleys, of how hard
it is to sustain joy.

Better questions might have been:
How do you cherish joy? How do you
remember it?

And if that moment was
full of joy, what joy
does this one hold?

The sun comes out.
Cobwebs in the hedge
are strung with bright pearls,

droplets that vanish
into air until the threads
become invisible again.

(Rudd, 2017)

This unpublished poem started as a theological reflection of a kind, on a conversation I recalled from a context of spiritual direction. My reflection began with wonder at the joy another person had discovered, and my own impulse to 'bottle' that joy and keep it going. Although I was unaware of this at the time, there is another poem which hovers behind this one: William Blake's four-line reflection, entitled 'Eternity' (Blake, 1972, 179):

He who binds to himself a joy
Does the winged life destroy
He who kisses the joy as it flies
Lives in eternity's sunrise

The first part of the poem leads me to an Ignatian reflection about consolation, that recollection and 'savouring' may be the way to reinforce the work of God in the heart. So far, I suppose all of this could have been done by writing in prose. The 'poetry moment' occurs in a *shift*, or *turn*, before the last two stanzas.

Walking in Wales in the early morning, a sea mist had closed in on the view until I could only see a few yards ahead. This maybe focused me in on the things that lay really close to me, particularly the spider webs in the hedgerow. These complex, fragile structures are normally unnoticed, but in the mist they had become extravagantly decorated with droplets of water that sparkled as they caught the light.

This image attached itself – that is the only way I can describe it, it wasn't at the conscious deliberate level – to the reflection on joy. Setting an image from the natural world in this context may initiate all kinds of conversations between the idea of sustaining joy and the 'world of the image'. In that world there are things that pass and fade, and that is what makes them beautiful. There is a dawning light of day which not only makes things visible but changes and transforms them:

> But the path of the righteous is like the light of dawn,
>   which shines brighter and brighter until full day.
>
> (Proverbs 4.18)

The concrete image, when it is accurately described, casts unexpected light on a process of reflection. The image is in no way worked up as an allegory of the idea – that is essentially a lifeless process. It is a perception, a shift of consciousness which allows paradox and indeterminacy to be expressed. It is a 'crack' in the discourse where 'the light gets in'.

This process opens us up to experience, but it also makes a deep interpersonal connection between writer and reader.

> One of the great functions of art is to help us imagine what it is like to be not ourselves, what it is like to be someone or something else, what it is like to live in another skin, what it is like to live in another body, and in that sense to surpass ourselves, to go out beyond ourselves.
>
> Adrienne Rich[1]

What's different about a poem?

So what are the characteristics of poetry that lend themselves to the process of theological reflection? Poems are significantly different from other forms of communication, in at least the following seven ways:

1 Poetry, like prose, is *about* stuff – it pays attention to the world. But it's also *about* itself. A poem pays attention to the language in which it is expressed. Even while it speaks it is listening, reflecting, to the texture of the words, to their layers of sound and meaning. It is a highly reflective attention – self-conscious, self-critical, listening for a particular kind of truth to be disclosed.

2 Poetry puts experience into a pattern. It finds a shape or form, to hold experience – which may have to do with making sense of it, or may point to another level of understanding. It is a kind of writing that is deeply committed to the discovery and expression of meaning. *All this has happened to me, but now it is held together on the page, and that in itself gives it a kind of meaning.*

3 Poetry, unlike prose, doesn't reach the edge of the page. It keeps stopping. It is broken speech, pausing, halting, taking a breath, allowing space for silence within the text. Line breaks, stanza breaks – all these are different kinds of hesitations. With every line break the poem keeps asking the question, as it progresses down the page: what catches my attention? What is real to me now? What is the shape of my experience? What meaning do I find? – questions that are certainly theological.

4 Poetry reaches out to recreate an experience in the mind or voice of the reader, it strives for the moment of recognition. It works with metaphor – literally 'carrying across' in profound communication. Somebody once said to me after a poetry reading, 'It makes pictures in my head.' According to Paul Ricoeur, metaphor is a site of unexpected and surprising changes in distance, and this gives it crucial importance in communication and interpretation. He defines metaphor as 'the bringing closer together of terms that, previously "remote", suddenly appear "close"' (Ricoeur, 2008, 9).

5 Poetry is encounter. 'Poetry', says Elizabeth Alexander, 'is the human voice, and are we not of interest to each other?' (Alexander, 2006, 28). A good poem allows me to draw near to another person, to move from I/It to I/Thou – in Buber's terms (2008) to encounter deeply. This is even effective outside the normal categories of space and time. A poem written long ago or far away can still reach me with startling immediacy.

6 Poetry is condensed – it whittles away any words or ideas that are not essential. It is always moving towards the essential – the heart of the matter.

7 Poetry prefers image to idea, it prefers the primary source to the secondary: because image is closer to what is real than any translation of it into ideas.

So, it may be possible to summarize the kind of thinking that takes place in a poem (both in the process of writing or the process of reading) and relate that to processes of theological reflection.

As soon as somebody writes a poem they are framing and selecting experience, reflecting on it, seeking to express it in the best words, introducing contemplative pauses (line breaks). And framed like this, a moment of experience becomes a kind of world of its own. It invites us in, and we experience it, we question, we wonder.

The thinking in a poem is not usually logical and linear, it is more associative – one idea suggests another, the door opens into somewhere different. Something new occurs.

If I can make a comparison with theological reflection, it is like the process of discovering the heart of the matter, and allowing that to become an image. If I can put it this way, a poem is *all* 'heart of the matter', and its normal currency is images, metaphors, seeing one thing in terms of another.

Metaphor

George Lakoff and Mark Johnson (2003), with their work on a therapeutic approach known as 'Clean Language', observe the way in which much of our language is already made up of metaphor – images that have been used to express ideas which now seem to carry no metaphoric charge at all. I used the word 'express' in that sentence without envisaging any of the physical imagery implied in the history of the word. As we describe our experience, we are always reaching for 'it's like …' 'as if' – in this we are making metaphor. The clean language approach listens carefully to the metaphors which occur in a client's account of their experience, then asks simple questions which, in the language of theological reflection, 'explore the world of the image'. This process of making and exploring metaphor is greatly enhanced by the experience of poetry. It trains the reader to listen for the nuances and possibilities of common language.

Metaphor-making is therefore crucial. According to James Olney (1981, 32), metaphor is above all else a way of knowing, which 'allows us to connect the known of ourselves to the unknown of the world'. This is, of course, far more than a development of the language: it affects the way the self is constituted or brought into being. Metaphor makes available 'new relational patterns' and 'simultaneously organizes the self into a new and richer entity; so that the old known self is joined to and transformed into the new, the hitherto unknown, self'.

So to write or read a poem is to engage in that sort of thinking, thinking that constantly leads us 'out of the box', but also sensitizes us to the language itself. It startles tired language into freshness and insight.

I would like to label all this as theological, either actual or potential, as I see theology as a reflection on the experience of life, and an encounter with its depth, its meaning, its mystery.

Rowan Williams (1999, xiii) identifies three styles of theology:

1 Celebratory – a theology that pays close attention to the world and what it is, looking for pattern and meaning. 'The seed moment is that element of celebration, or wonder at where we are – joyful wonder at the heart of it.'
2 Communicative – that tries to say something about the world that makes sense to somebody else.
3 Critical – the self-reflective, conscious of language, questioning.

So, here is a first attempt to look at poetry in these categories, to map them on to my seven characteristics of poetry:

1 Poetry attends to the world and the voice (celebratory).
2 Poetry finds a shape to hold experience (celebratory).
3 Poetry is broken speech (communicative).
4 Poetry reaches out (communicative).
5 Poetry is encounter (communicative).
6 Poetry is condensed (critical).
7 Poetry prefers image to idea (critical).

The Emmaus journey to recognition

I would like to suggest the familiar story of the road to Emmaus (Luke 24.13–35) as a parable of theological reflection. It is a powerful symbol of the road that leads us through our thinking together to a place where we recognize Christ. It is a paradigm of so much of our experience. It is the journey from sadness and doubt to a new kind of joy – a journey that we often long for, and sometimes realize.

Every now and then a group theological reflection seems to enter a different place, it seems as if it catches fire. It becomes an encounter. It becomes a recognition of Christ. How does this happen?

In Luke's account, while the two disciples were talking (*homileo* – conversing with each other) and discussing (*suzeteo* – searching together, trying to get to the bottom of the matter) Jesus came and walked with them.

Isn't this what we do, in our groups, in our reading? A theological reflection is often a discussion that comes out of a tension, or something that doesn't make sense. Something is not quite right, something has disappointed us.

In the world of poetry, it is a commonplace that a lot of poems are miserable. Maybe the reason is that when a person is happy they just get on and enjoy it. But when they are sad they become reflective and are tempted to write about it. Maybe the same applies to theological reflection? We find it much easier to stop and think when something stops us, or disturbs us. Anyway, that's what these two disciples were doing: 'We had hoped that he was the one ...'

So Luke continues: 'Jesus himself came near and went with them, but their eyes were kept from recognizing him' (15–16).

It is an astonishing turn of events. In the middle of their miserable discussion Jesus himself shows up. It may seem a rather pious assertion, but I really believe it to be true: that in our discussions, in our reflections, in our search for truth, Jesus often walks beside us and frequently we do not recognize him. As the narrative continues, Jesus redescribes their conversation to them. And he says to them, 'What words (*logos* – conclusion) are you discussing (*antiballete* – what are these words that you have been pitching back and forth to each other?) with each other while you walk along?'

It is possible that we need to change the quality of our discourse, moving away from that kind of 'discussion' before we are open to the presence of Christ. What the 'ballistic' discussion lacks is any sense of attention, of presence to one another. It's not a contest.

So the text Luke offers suggests three distinct 'openings':

- Jesus opened the scriptures (27, 32).
- Jesus opened their eyes (31).
- Jesus opened their minds (45). 'Then he opened their minds to understand the scriptures ...'

As Jesus talked with them on the road he 'opened' the scriptures to them (27, 32). This was not literally, of course, none of them had a Bible – but it is worth pausing a moment in the world of the image. In every synagogue, the scriptures, the scrolls of the law and the prophets, were kept safe in a box – but to read the scriptures this had to be opened. Then the scroll itself had to be unrolled, *opened out*. This gives a depth and nuance to the meaning of 'opening the scriptures', making the text visible, making it possible to read and understand.

One person can 'open' the words of Scripture for another: the hermeneutic, the opening of understanding, because unless it is opened the text would seem to have no effect. The holiness of the holy book is not because it is a special or beautiful artefact, but in the way in which it is 'opened' into our lives and hearts.

So what is it that 'closes' the text to us? There may be many barriers of culture, language, ideas. We may bring to the text a host of set patterns of thinking, our cultural expectations. We come with the rigidity of our theological positions.

This may be another reason why poetry has some importance. In my experience, understanding poetry helps me to understand and respond to the text of the Bible. It opens doors for me. The practice of poetry leads us to the vital process of attention – close reading, reading that allows us to be *spoken to* by the text.

For Luke, in this narrative, it is vital for this hermeneutic process to lead to recognition. It's not enough to criticize, evaluate and analyse the text: there has to be a point of recognition, of opened eyes (31), a deeper kind of knowing. This in turn leads to an opening of the mind (45), 'Then he opened their minds to understand the scriptures.'

The experience of the risen Christ is a constant and endless opening. Jesus is the one who says 'Ephphatha ... Be opened' (Mark 7.34). This is an experience which opens, and opens – opens ears and eyes, opens tables, opens closed social systems. It is the opening of an unlimited and inclusive kingdom that upends the closed systems of this world.

As the disciples approached their house, Jesus 'walked ahead as if he were going on' (24.28); Jesus is 'always going further'. Wherever we are, whatever we know or understand, Jesus is always ahead, always going further.

> He is such a fast
> God, always before us and
> leaving as we arrive.

(Thomas, 1993, 364)

But then comes the unexpected moment. He lifts the bread, and we recognize him. May we receive and cherish these moments, these recognitions. *Something understood.*

Storying the self

Rowan Williams, for instance, in *Lost Icons* (2000, 114), offers a delineation of the way in which *soul* develops. His account is intricate and integrative: firmly located within the Christian tradition but robust enough to retain its relevance in a secular context. The human self is not a given, but is continually created – as Williams describes it – by reflection, by telling its own story. It is a destabilized self, a self which is never static, always coming into being. The world that a person perceives and recognizes is immediately organized and captured in narrative, and outside this narrative there is no self:

> The self lives and moves in, only in, acts of telling – in the time taken to set out and articulate a memory, the time that is a kind of representation (always partial, always skewed) of the time my material and mental life has taken, the time that has brought me here. To step aside from this kind of telling and retelling, this always shifting and growing representation of the past, is in effect to abandon thinking itself or language itself.

Such a view of the self, *storying* itself into being, has an immediate implication for the writer. It suggests that to engage creatively with the language as a writer can be much more than a journey into language; it is a way to explore the meanings and boundaries of the self.

As Laurel Richardson recovered from a devastating accident, she found that writing became her way to reconstruct her life:

> Writing was the method through which I constituted the world and reconstituted myself. Writing became my principal tool through which I learned about myself and the world. I wrote so I would have a life. (2001, 33)

This experience led her to value what she calls 'writing-stories' as an effective methodology for research, and she continues: 'I write because I want to find something out. I write in order to learn something that I did not know before I wrote it' (35). Such 'storying of the self' is a common human experience, but the poet is a special, intensified case of this because of the attentive reflexivity required in the art of poetry. The poet's work explicitly consists in making meaning, paying attention precisely and specifically to the weight and texture of every word, as well as to the many ways in which they interact. It is: 'The process of "making" a self by constructing a story that is always being retold ...' (Williams, 2000, 114).

Quoting Walter Davies, Williams asserts that the self is not a fixity, but only 'becomes' a self through the shifting process of self-reflection:

> [...] a self is only really definable in the act of self-questioning; reflecting on the self can't be a way of thinking about an 'item' that will stay in focus while we look at it. The act of questioning is the act in which the self is itself.

> (2000, 146)

Again, the persona of a poet exemplifies this. It expresses itself through a personal 'voice' – unique to each poet. This voice only exists as it interrogates experience; and as it develops, it learns to detach itself deliberately from any externally determined context. The power of the lyric voice – and this is accomplished by its choice of words, by its artfulness – is its ability to convince the reader that an encounter between persons is taking place, to create the illusion of a realized self, to summon a kind of presence.

Note

1 https://anthonywilsonpoetry.com/2016/01/29/one-of-the-great-functions-of-art-by-adrienne-rich/

10

Theological reflection as praxis

JUDITH EVANS

I had some initial reluctance in being asked to contribute to a book on theological reflection, particularly one that favours a specific model. In terms of the theological training of lay ministers in my diocese, I have successfully argued that theological reflection not be taught as a discrete entity in one academic module, studying one or more models and applying to contextual issues. I would argue that the whole emphasis needs to be altered and instead of theological reflection being viewed as something one does and applies – praxis reflection should be the pedagogical norm (Jenkins, 2017, 115) – *reflecting theologically* needs to become the norm and part and parcel of who we are.

In my experience it would seem that theological reflection is one of the areas being squeezed in theological education in the UK,[1] and its value as an integrating factor within theological education is questioned, which has a twofold inference for practice. First, that its impact on practical theology and the impact in the day-to-day life of the parish is not being recognized, and second the importance of *reflecting theologically* by both lay and ordained people is not being encouraged or modelled. Theological reflection needs to be overtly affirmed as a practice which all in the Church undertake in every aspect of church life: liturgical practice; ecclesiology; development of theology; implications for doctrinal change; pastoral care of young people and families, pastoral care of the elderly; funeral ministry – before and after the funeral – every aspect of our corporate church lives. While those undertaking a ministerial position in the church have a specific role in leading and enabling theological reflection, its rightful place is as an ethos, a way of thinking about how we approach every aspect of church life and not something done in isolation and applied to a specific issue for either a practical application or as an academic exercise. *Thinking theologically* should not be regarded as a purely clerical paradigm but one that equally belongs to lay people, completely rooted in everyday practice in the church, and part and parcel of our lives as people of God in the world. I would therefore argue that *thinking theologically* should not be sidelined as a series of models that are increasingly given just a passing nod in academia, but instead given huge prominence from the outset – for anyone wanting to become involved in church life at any level, as the way we think about and make decisions on any aspect of church life.

A parochial example

Perhaps the best way I can illustrate this is by looking at an experience I had in parish ministry. At the end of a PCC meeting in October 2012, the vicar raised an issue. He had been contacted by someone who didn't live in the parish but had a qualifying connection and who was a divorcee, to ask if another minister could conduct their remarriage in our church. The position at that time was that, due to the vicar's own feelings on the subject, no remarriage in church was permissible. This question, however, came at a time when the incumbent was beginning to discern whether his position should change. He therefore raised it at the end of the meeting. A heated debate soon arose, with extremes of feelings being voiced both for and against the idea of remarriage in church. I therefore proposed that we end the discussion as it was then late, everyone was tired, and it was not an appropriate forum to continue debate, and that I research the topic, present my findings to the PCC, and we debate the issue again. What came across immediately was that this was a question that elicited a passionate response and great division. The response was either a 'from the heart' response – it was wrong to divorce and remarry under any circumstances, marriage is ordained by God and is for life, versus why should people be punished by the Church for making a mistake. Moreover, there was felt to be a great injustice in that people could be married having clearly lived together and had children, not necessarily from the same partner, but were treated far better and very differently from those who had tried to do the right thing and legitimize their union through marriage which had subsequently failed. The two extremes were swift to talk about right and wrong, justice and injustice, but with no *theological* underpinning to their thesis.

The issue had first been raised in the PCC some years before when the General Synod meeting of 2002 changed the Church's position, stating:

> The Church accepts that, in exceptional circumstances, a divorced person may marry again in church during the lifetime of a former spouse.[2]

I understand that the issue caused great tension when discussed at that time, with the PCC secretary (who was divorced and in a new relationship) being so upset at the decision to stand by the incumbent's views and not remarry people that she resigned on the spot. As one PCC member noted, ten years down the line, it seemed right to revisit this question again – but immediately tensions and completely divergent views were expressed, which were sometimes unhelpful to debate and understanding.

The presentation I gave took place on a Saturday morning a few weeks later and it was pleasing to see a nearly full PCC in attendance while the two who had given apologies had asked for the presentation and notes to be forwarded to them. This was the beginning of a journey where we explored in some depth each of the four sources: Tradition (biblical and ecclesial), Experience, Culture and Position. This covered the history of marriage over the centuries and the move from church to state control; the different models of acceptable marriage in the Old Testament; the change in marital status that Christ and Paul referred to in the New Testament; and the cultural changes in this country that had made divorce and re-marriage increase. Following the presentation there was a good debate where parts of what had been said were highlighted, discussed and clarified – the atmosphere was good. A full copy of the presentation notes was given to all attendees to take home and address.

It was evident as the debate took place, that although the same parties were present who had got so angry and upset at the original PCC meeting where the issue was raised, they had come with a calmer mindset and were more prepared to listen to one another's views. What also became clear as that discussion evolved was that the premise of debate had slightly altered. No longer was this a discussion on whether another minister could conduct a remarriage in our church, it was on whether remarriages should take place. This change of emphasis in the debate was apparent in all parties, including the incumbent – formerly entrenched views were beginning to change. And it was the language used to express that change that was so important – rights and wrongs, justice and injustice, was being replaced by biblical allusions and a sense of where God was in all this. They were beginning to reflect, think and talk theologically. Without being taught any theory or being asked to apply a model to their thoughts, feelings and constructs – they were beginning to *reflect theologically.*

Over the next few weeks I visited each PCC member in ones and twos to interview them about the issue. Notes were taken and presented back to the PCC at the end of the process in a précis form and in a way that no contributor could be identified. It was quite humbling to see the care and attention given to the comprehensive presentation transcript which was a lengthy and theologically challenging document. Yet they had taken pains to engage with it properly, commenting on parts, quoting others – they were highlighted, covered with notes, and particular attention had been given to the biblical passages and their exegesis.

There was an attention to the *theological* underpinning of the various aspects and an honest appraisal by some that they had assumed that the

Bible gives a clear view on our modern interpretation of marriage and realized now that it was not that simple. The modern marriage service reflecting the covenantal relationship of God's love for us[3] was a new insight for most. This led to a lot of discussion on how covenants can sometimes be broken, and remade. I am often wary of images in terms of theological reflection as they can divert discussion down a particular route and can be open to manipulation by poor facilitation, particularly if there are other processes at work in the group. For a couple of people, however, the power of an image was a pivotal point in the process for them. Although elsewhere in this book (see the discussion on critical distance in Chapter 3) we would counsel against having an image too close to the original question – in this case it would prove powerful for one interviewee to have the image of a bruised, broken and battered wife in his mind. He had been so adamantly against there ever being any grounds for divorce that could be advocated by the Church and yet, as he said, 'That image haunted me for days. What was I saying by taking the stance I have? Why was I condemning someone to a life of brokenness and despair with no chance of redemption through another relationship?'

Throughout the presentation and subsequent debate and interviews, I strove not to impart my own position on this, but posed questions that offered another viewpoint that might challenge the listener, and asked a series of open questions that would need the respondent to think about and be able to present clearly their position.

I think it was beneficial to leave a period for reflection between the presentation and the interview stage and a further period between interviews and the reconvened discussion at the PCC. One of the issues I have experienced in teaching the four-source model is the insistence – usually imposed by the limits of class or workshop – that they are time bound, deeming it somehow advantageous to get the whole reflection completed within an hour and a half. I don't see the benefit in this and, as someone who is naturally a reflective thinker and needs time to process the multi-layered amount of information being presented, through both verbal and non-verbal cues, I like to take time. For big issues, that should be reflected theologically; I believe it is vital that we take time or risk manipulating the group into an insight that the convenor/facilitator of the reflective process can want to achieve from the outset.

Building in these opportunities for discussion, followed by reflection, enabled the parties to see things from the perspective of others. It was noticeable that those who had attended the debate and were available for interview were far more able to see things from the perspective of others. Initially some had been so caught up with the politics and emotion of what was happening they couldn't gain a larger view. Through this whole project I learned that by slowing down and seeing things from another perspective greater clarity and learning can occur. The semi-structured interviews were a useful way of teasing out of people their own perspective, but also to get them to discuss others without being wary of attack. One of the most illuminating of these was with the incumbent who was now clearly in a very different place than when the subject was initially mooted.

It is vital for anyone in a ministry role to be open to the views of others. It is important to sometimes be able to passionately argue for something we believe in, but not to close our ears to the insights that others can provide, their perspective, their context. It was a privilege to discuss this issue with so many, both in a group and on a one-to-one basis, and witness through this dialogue the thoughtfulness, prayerfulness and humility many members of the PCC had and the paradigm shift some were willing to make, even though they found doing so very difficult, taking them away from where they had stood previously on this issue. What was most illuminating, however, was how things had been viewed from a largely pragmatic way by the lay members of the PCC and that they had, prior to this process, viewed theology as purely the preserve of the ministry team. The final discussion back at the full PCC meeting led to the conclusion that in some circumstances, provided the incumbent had completed the necessary paperwork provided by the Church for this, satisfied himself that lessons had been learned, that the couple wishing to be remarried were not the cause of the previous marriage breakdown, that remarriage would be permitted in our church. Individual experience was of course crucial in this, but as the process unfolded there came an appreciation of the other areas too.

The more important conclusion perhaps was a corporate understanding of how we are all called to make decisions not based on instinct, but on a thoughtful and informed basis, and how we were just beginning our journey of reflecting theologically together. It identified to many in the group the danger of assuming that theological beliefs and ecclesial identity are shared by all in the room – in reality, a far more nuanced picture emerged. It also made clear to me that practical theology is not the preserve of theologians and academics but is absolutely rooted in praxis and is something for every one of us to participate in.

Notes

1 And not just here. See, for example, John Paver in Australia (2006, 126–7) whose curriculum proposal envisioning theological reflection as a method of integration for theological education in the Uniting Church Theological College (Parkville, Victoria, Australia) was never accepted by the members of his faulty.

2 This useful summary is contained in the *Marriage in Church after Divorce: Form and Explanatory Statement* available from Church House Publishing (2003).

3 See Timothy and Kathy Keller, *The Meaning of Marriage: Facing the Complexities of Commitment with the Wisdom of God* (2011).

11

Theological action research

GARY O'NEILL

We believe that the four-source model of theological reflection has been overlooked by many practical theologians. The research undertaken by the co-operative inquiry groups and our experience of teaching at All Saints convinces us that this model is worthy of wider dissemination. Furthermore, there has been a growing trend among some in practical theology to assert that research undertaken in this field is a form of action research based on the essential nature of practical theology. Embracing the argument that practical theology is an outcome-oriented discipline, John Swinton and Harriet Mowat in their work *Practical Theology and Qualitative Research* made the claim that practical theology *is* action research (2006, 255). With the reprinting of this very successful text ten years later, their conclusion remains the same, suggesting – since they eschew the option to amend their text – they hold the view vehemently (2016, 261).

As we indicated in Chapter 1, the dominant theological reflection model used in this country is the pastoral cycle, and one prominent proponent of this model is Helen Cameron. In this chapter we examine the way in which she uses the pastoral cycle and explore her claim to be undertaking theological action research. To accomplish this, five books are considered in publication date order. This chapter was written primarily by me, so the precise detail of some of the arguments are attributable to me alone; the rest of the chapter is a first-person account to make that evident.

This chapter does not seek to critique or review these books as a whole; rather, I seek to test the assertion that what is being undertaken is theological action research. Helen Cameron is a respected practitioner in the field of practical theology and this is neither a review of her work nor an assessment of her contribution to the field. To revisit my modified version of Ruard Ganzevoort in Chapter 2, I am a player coach critiquing the coach of another team in her use of the off-side trap in football, or a defensive zone in netball, or offensive field placements in cricket. In addition, at the end of the chapter I demonstrate the usefulness of 'theology in four voices' and how the four-source model complements this.

Since I am ultimately critical of her use of the pastoral cycle, and her claim to be conducting action research, I contrast other practitioners who use the *pastoral circle* (see page 165) before suggesting how the models might converse. I conclude that the use of the pastoral cycle in the UK has perhaps lost its cutting edge, and if both models were to consider each other's discipline and approach, there could be rich benefits for action research in practical theology.

Resourcing Mission (2010)

Resourcing Mission and *Talking about God in Practice* were both published in 2010. The former is based on two arguments, of which the first is:

> Churches can think about change theologically using a method [*sic*] called 'the pastoral cycle' that leads from reflection to action.
>
> (Cameron, 2010, x)

Helen Cameron goes on to briefly introduce the reader to the pastoral cycle but without giving a detailed explanation or description; she relies upon the reader having access to two other sources if a detailed approach is required (Ballard and Pritchard, 2006; Wijsen, Henriot and Mejía, 2005). Cameron claims that her work

> ... looks at the challenges of making use of the Bible and Christian doctrine within the pastoral cycle.
>
> (2010, 1)

However, her lack of detail and a reluctance to 'show her working' hide the reasons for her choices both of Scripture and doctrine in the seven worked examples that follow. These examples explore eleven passages of Scripture and six different doctrinal areas. Of the eleven scriptural passages, I observe that all are from the New Testament, all bar one from the Gospels, and she uses Matthew eight times. Why is there nothing from the Old Testament? I am not suggesting that her choices are poor, rather that no explanation is offered for the choices. One of my concerns with Laurie Green's work (1990) is the way his method makes connections to Scripture with 'intuitive leaps' with no indication offered to the reader of how this actually happens. In describing the flow of a theological reflection group using the pastoral cycle he states:

Thus far the group has been intent on making intuitive leaps across the hermeneutical gap between our own culture and that of the Bible and other treasures from our Christian heritage.

(2009, 98)

Helen Cameron appears to be following suit. She also declares that reasons will be offered for selecting particular doctrines (2010, 16), yet this is not self-evident, and within her summaries of complex chapters of the primary source (Hodgson and King, 2008) it is not easy to identify the provenance of ideas or concepts.

I would suggest that the reason for this unexplained treatment of Scripture and doctrine is her unacknowledged assumption that the pastoral cycle is 'tried and tested' (2010, 17). It is indeed well used – this is one of my concerns – and this can easily lead to an uncritical use. In one short sentence there is, arguably, acknowledgement that there are critics of the pastoral cycle (2010, 10), and there is some irony in the fact that the one source she cites for this critique is the same source readers are signposted to for a description of the model, namely the work of Frans Wijsen et al. (2005).

Talking about God in Practice (2010)

Theological reflection and action research are two of my research interests, so my expectations were high for a book written by a team of practical theologians (Helen Cameron, Deborah Bhatti, Catherine Duce, James Sweeney and Clare Watkins) from the ARCS project (Action Research: Church and Society) with the subtitle *Theological Action Research and Practical Theology* (2010, iii).

I concur with the writers that one of the most significant developments in practical theology is theological reflection, but I would refute the assertion that 'central to these methods is the pastoral cycle' (2010, 27). It may be central to many models but not all, as is implied. Judith Thompson, for example, organizes models into five different categories (Thompson, Pattison and Thompson, 2008) and Pete Ward offers a further six ways of doing theological reflection which do not use the pastoral cycle (2017, 102–14).

Commenting on the tendency for practical theologians to begin with experience, they demonstrate a narrowness to their own research reading:

Developments of the pastoral cycle into different models of theological reflection have led to a recognition that there may be times when other starting places may be appropriate. For example, among Killen and de

Beer's nine processes of personal theological reflection[1] are examples of starting with scripture reading, with a doctrine of faith, with a cultural text, and with an everyday object.

(2010, 28)

This is a slightly cursory reading of the text (none of the examples starts from doctrine) and betrays a merely casual acquaintance with Patricia Killen and John de Beer's work, which is not based on the pastoral cycle but on the work of James and Evelyn Whitehead, who introduced a three-source model of reflection in which there is no reference to the pastoral cycle. The Whiteheads cite Tillich, Lonergan and Tracy, who influence their work and the tradition in the United States of Clinical Pastoral Education (CPE) combined with the use of case studies (1980, 1–4). None of these voices are cited in relation to the pastoral cycle in the work of Paul Ballard and John Pritchard, whose version of the pastoral cycle Cameron et al. refer to (2010, 28).

The most extravagant claim the authors make for this publication is that their book marks the first time action research has appeared in practical theology (2010, 39). I would refute that claim by revisiting the definition and understanding of action research and bringing those insights to bear on the methodology employed in *Talking about God in Practice*. There are at least five areas of the ARCS's research methodology which I would question.

Biographical detail

As I have indicated when introducing myself as researcher and writer, it is my practice to reveal a significant amount of biographical detail because there are many factors which have an influence on the way in which I perceive things. An understanding of a person's background is helpful when in a face-to-face conversation; in the written medium, if the reader does not share the experience you are describing, then background information is even more important and gives the reader insight with which to weigh the content of what they read. Other than their names and roles, the authors of *Talking about God in Practice* tell us nothing of their background, theology, politics, affiliations or convictions. This is not something which would be regarded as normative in action research. Jean McNiff, in her most recent work on writing and doing action research, offers several pages about her background (2014, 8–9) and Ernest Stringer's handbook on action research threads stories from his experience throughout the text as biographical bulletins (2007, 17).

Positionality

As indicated above when outlining my own research approach, Kathryn Herr and Gary Anderson offer a continuum for researchers which provides a language to describe the researcher's role or positionality (2005, 29).

Cameron et al. root their definition of action research in the work of Danny Burns (2007) and Davydd Greenwood and Morten Levin (2007), summarizing it as

- a partnership
- a process
- a conversation
- a way of knowing

... between participants in an organization who are interested in researching their practice or solving a problem and researchers who have an interest in what can be learned from practice.

(Cameron et al., 2010, 36)

They then go on to value their own role as outsider researchers because in their commitment to insiders they can 'challenge their thinking' (2010, 37). In cherry-picking their sources Cameron et al. misunderstand the essence of action research.

Peter Reason and Hilary Bradbury make a point of emphasizing that action research is something that is undertaken *with* people.[2] It is clear from the chapters describing the three case studies – on research in a parish, diocese and faith-based agency – that the researching team is one stage removed from the action. The data collection is undertaken by an ARCS researcher in the parish, a volunteer co-researcher in the diocese, and jointly by an ARCS fieldworker and a Housing Justice employee in the agency. This means that when the insider team gathers with ARCS outsiders it is not unusual for there to be only one person present who has first-hand experience of the participants in the research.

Morten Levin, in writing further on the need to educate action researchers in both the principles and practicalities of their discipline, emphasizes strongly the necessity for action research to include action and research.

First, proficiency is needed in order to concretely and practically work with social change in order to solve participants' pertinent problems. Second, skills are needed to enable creation of sustainable cogenerative learning processes involving both problem owners and researchers in the same learning cycle.

(2008, 669)

These researchers are not part of the research experience, and since so little is revealed about them it is difficult to infer what determines their choices.

Multiple cycles

It has been accepted for a long time in action research that it is good practice to have as many research cycles as possible; this is an insight going back nearly 70 years to the work of one of the forerunners in the field, Kurt Lewin, as Peter Reason and Hilary Bradbury indicate (2008, 4). Part of the culture of action research is that one cycle generates data for a subsequent cycle so that co-researchers break new ground together. In the ARCS account two of the case studies have two cycles and a third only one cycle; however, the writers give the impression (for example, in the faith-based agency) that the second cycle often involved different people. This is therefore not a cycle in which people are co-researching because the make-up of the groups is different. There is little sense here that the groups are developing.

Interviews

The data in the parish case study is gathered by interviews, the diocesan case used both a questionnaire and interviews, and the faith-based agency used focus groups. It is difficult to see how action research principles of democracy, openness, the sharing of data and a sense of working with people can operate in these contexts. Interviews and focus groups are a recognized way of gathering data, but do they meet the criteria of action research if the participants have no control over the questions or what happens to the data? Involvement in focus groups and other small group activities might be a precursor to involving people as co-researchers as, for example, in Meghna Guhathakurta's work with the sweeper community in Bangladesh. Here a number of approaches were used to 'foreground them into the existing development discourse' before she welcomed them into the participatory action research (PAR) project (2008, 513). Alternatively, interviews and focus groups might be part of a much larger project which itself is considered to be participatory so, for example, in Lai Fong Chiu's research, the involvement of bilingual community health educators in the designing of questionnaires is seen by her as participatory involvement of co-researchers (2008, 543), even though the questionnaire is not. Again, there is a sense here that people are drawn into an increasingly participatory role and that the action research principle of orientation to inquiry demands the researcher encourage this: 'PAR's relationship to participants goes beyond a willingness to be interviewed' (2008, 541).

This is not manifest in these ARCS case studies nor by inference in the other 14 research projects in the appendix, which indicate that interviews, participant observation, phone calls, focus groups and reflective writing are listed as research methods (Cameron et al., 2010, 156–9).

Prayer

Action research would not normally be characterized by a claim to include prayer in research since the field, wide though it may be, does not enjoy a strong faith-based stream, though an exception might be John Heron and Gregg Lahood's research on the 'in between', being both a 'spiritual practice' and 'sacred science' (2008, 339), and David Coghlan's work on Ignatian spirituality (2005). However, Cameron et al. make a claim for *theological* action research in a self-evaluation of their work:

> Fundamentally TAR is built on the conviction that the Holy Spirit is moving Christ's people to an even deeper understanding of faith; and that this 'theology' is before us, waiting to be 'seen' or recognized.
>
> (2010, 148)

There is no mention of prayer in their work, and this conviction about the Holy Spirit is not developed, nor is any evidence cited from their research. How can action research, an orientation to inquiry, be a theological orientation to inquiry without any discussion of the way in which the Holy Spirit is seen to work in the process and without any discussion about the way in which the participants access God?

My observation is that the method ARCS employs as outlined in *Talking about God in Practice* – researching on people; not offering any information on researchers; a limited number of research cycles; an emphasis on interviews and focus groups and no mention of prayer – is more accurately described as a form of *qualitative* rather than action research and struggles to be theological by its own criteria. The authors acknowledge the need for people 'trained in the design and execution of qualitative research' (2010, 78) but I am not convinced that they appreciate just how much this dependence skews the ethos of the research away from genuine participation.

Elaine Graham

The publication of *Talking about God in Practice* prompted Elaine Graham to examine the claim that practical theology ought to be regarded as a form of action research (2013). In her survey of the field beyond practical theology, Elaine Graham recognizes a commitment to *reflexivity* by which the researchers are themselves subject to critical scrutiny; however, in Cameron she sees a failure of the researchers to place themselves under this kind of scrutiny. Graham says that their research

> ... fails to address the 'positionality' of Cameron and her team, who remain resolutely 'off the page' in terms of any declaration or exploration of their own reflexivity.
>
> (2013, 164)

In surveying work in practical theology over the last 30 years that might be considered as action research, she concludes that,

> whilst there is attention to the subjectivity or positionality of the researcher in these studies, most of them stop short of any kind of first person reflexivity – in Herr and Anderson's terms [2005, 31], the researcher is more off, than on, the page. Furthermore, whilst most have attempted to undertake some kind of consultancy with their subjects, there is little true collaboration in terms of research design.
>
> (2013, 169)

I read this article only after I had completed my co-operative inquiry research. It endorses my approach to being as open as possible with myself, my co-researchers, critical friends and readers of this book in order to invite critical feedback. All those involved in the research had access to our agreed accounts and were offered earlier drafts of my writing, looping back with their comments; colleagues and students at All Saints have seen successive drafts of Chapter 3; and those in the EfM community have also been using the model. I believe this final written work stands as testimony to my practice of openness and collaboration.

Theological Reflection for Human Flourishing (2012)

The primary authors of this work, John Reader and Victoria Slater, headed up by Helen Cameron, are all members of the Oxford Centre of Ecclesiology and Practical Theology (OxCEPT). The first of two purposes for the book is to 'provide an example of a process of theological reflection and offer a commentary on the practical problems encountered' (Cameron et al., 2012, ix). The title of the work is intriguing – the authors give no explicit reason for the title, but as a practical theologian who has tried to immerse myself in the language and culture of action research, I cannot help but think they are borrowing an image from action research. In what is still predominantly either a humanist field (or if faith-based then the faith aspect is often played down or ignored) 'flourishing' is a positive and encouraging term which is used to describe the well-being of humanity both locally and globally. It is used frequently when discussing the outcome of action research. In the family of practices description from Peter Reason and Hilary Bradbury (see pages 19–20) it occurs twice in bullets two and four: 'relationships ... in which dialogue and development can flourish' and 'concerning the flourishing of human persons' (2008, 3 and 4). They see the initiation of action research as being 'driven by personal commitments to human flourishing' (2008, 11). Its use in practical theology is unusual and some, like Maureen Miner, would say that 'religious accounts of flourishing are unpopular in our times' (Miner, Dowson and Devenish, 2012, ix). I infer, therefore, that the use of the term 'flourishing' by Cameron et al. is deliberate.

As the lead editor Helen Cameron carries with her some of the incorrect assumptions made in earlier work and once again claims that most models of theological reflection have been developed from the pastoral cycle (Cameron et al., 2012, 3).

Unlike previous works, the book offers a fuller description of the steps of the pastoral cycle, and there is some development here as they are listed in eight steps (2012, 5–6). Five chapters of the book are dedicated to initiating the theological reflection ('triggering the conversation'), describing the experiences ('encounters') of participants, exploring the experiences, engaging with Scripture and learning from the encounters.

One of the dilemmas of reporting on research is how to strike a balance between giving the reader enough information to have a flavour of the research and not overwhelming the reader with detail, so one can have some sympathy for Cameron and her colleagues. However, in trying to assess what actually happened in the theological reflections and the sense in which this is action research, I can only note that extraordinarily little information is given, and the reader is left to make a few inferences from small scraps of data. There is a great deal we do not know.

We do know that the event was publicized and lasted 48 hours and was to be an 'action learning' event (2012, xxii) – no explanation or definition is given for an action learning event and there is no indication of the number of contact hours assigned to the event. Although 15 names are acknowledged as participants (2012, vii) we do not know where they came from, which reflection group they participated in, or how they felt about the process they had been involved in. One can infer from the acknowledgements that only 20 per cent of the participants were women. Little more is known of the researchers, who again remain firmly off the page except for a couple of random autobiographical 'resonances' (2012, 17). We do not know how the data was gathered or what agreement the participants came to over its use or any issues of confidentiality.

In turning to what contribution to knowledge Cameron et al. might offer about theological reflection, the reader is once again left to make inferences rather than offered credible detail. In the chapter on theological reflection, claims are made about the Holy Spirit and prayer which are not followed through. We are told that the 'Holy Spirit will continually reveal new things if we dare to look' but we are not told how the participants achieved this (2012, 8). In steps three to five there is a hint that prayer is used to reveal insight (2012, 6) and we are later informed that it is at the heart of theological reflection (2012, 9) – did prayer actually happen or is this wishful thinking? Of obvious interest to this researcher is the role of the authors (or others) as facilitators in the event – we are told briefly what a 'good facilitator' (2012, 7) might do, but nothing is expanded on. In the introduction the authors hope that 'the book will be an encouragement to those who facilitate theological reflection' (2012, xiii) – I am disappointed rather than encouraged. Given that this was an action learning event[3] I find it telling that there are no sources on the skill or discipline of facilitating experiential work in the final bibliography.

The most serious misstep is the engagement with Scripture; it must be said that, though surprised by what happened, the authors are honest about the difficulties. The authors recognize that their 'expectation that participants would readily turn to the Bible proved faulty' (2012, 74). In their conclusion they admit that this 'could be viewed as a derailment'. What may be considered helpful is that both the primary authors and Christopher Rowland see part of the problem as stemming from the way in which the Bible is perceived in the wider church (2012, 119). It is one answer, but it places the answer 'out there' – that is, it is not an admission that there is a weakness in the pastoral cycle itself. Why not move to a subsequent cycle of research, or initiate a new inquiry group, which would research how to improve connections with Scripture within the pastoral cycle? The fact that the authors do not make any suggestions along these lines confirms that this is more of a one-off event searching for the kind of theological insight that might make a good book, rather than the action research orientation to inquiry which would seek further participatory research.

It is astonishing that the authors, in writing up the event, appear to lack any reflexive insight on how intimidating the very presence in the room of an Oxford Professor of Exegesis of Holy Scripture (to give him his full title) might be for many people of faith. Furthermore, what does the very act of inviting the professor say about the authors' confidence in the pastoral cycle to be able to make connections with the Judeo-Christian tradition?

Researching Practice in Ministry and Mission (2013)

Helen Cameron and Catherine Duce, in this latest collaboration, express a concern that they may be 'too honest' and worry that people will not think they can learn anything from 'two research practitioners who have made so many mistakes' (2013, xxii). Given my comments on previous work about authors being 'off the page' it is encouraging to see that the writers this time introduce themselves. However, in the three pages they devote to this task the reader still gains little insight into how these two writers think and feel. The information is more at a professional biography surface level of roles undertaken and positions held, not meeting the criteria suggested by Nod Miller (see page 18).

A quote on the back of the book by John Swinton summarizing its approach is revealing: 'engaging in qualitative research' – where has action research gone?

In summary, the authors appear to have stepped back from their commitment to theological action research. Their previous work (2010) is only flagged up as an example of action research when comparing methodologies (32). They make unsupported assumptions that participant observation is action research (59), and while implying that interviews *can* be action research, they suggest this is 'Ill-advised' for MA students (82). Furthermore, the chapter on focus groups implies they are a form of qualitative research (111). Taken together, these three elements significantly weaken any case which they might have previously put for theological action research (Cameron, 2010; Cameron et al., 2012) because both these works rely heavily on work done in the ARCS, which favours interviews and focus groups.

Just Mission (2015)

In this most recent work Helen Cameron writes alone and attempts to provide a catalyst for local churches to become more involved in issues of justice both in their locality and nationally. This is not a book which intends to promote theological action research, nor does it overtly advocate use of the pastoral cycle; however, it undoubtedly flows from her continued interest in human flourishing rooted in a desire for a 'good society' and is of interest to me because of her recent track record. She introduces the 'justice-seeking cycle' as a model having similarity to the pastoral cycle (2015, 29–30) with four steps rather than the developed eight of earlier work (Cameron et al., 2012, 5–6). She continues to be defensive of the criticism that theology can simply be just a step in the pastoral cycle and her argument that God is present in every step if the 'local church becomes a fertile soil cultivating those who seek justice' is unsubstantiated (2015, 30). This weak defence is further undermined by a later admission that a team involved in the justice-seeking cycle may early on in the process have already resolved what action to take, so that engaging with the Christian tradition may feel 'artificial or unnecessary' (2015, 60). There then follows further reference to the difficulties she and her colleagues experienced with participants engaging with Scripture in the action learning event described in earlier work (Cameron et al., 2012).

The stepping away from both a claim for theological action research and the advocacy of the pastoral cycle of *Talking about God in Practice* now seems complete. It is as if in getting her fingers burned through the action learning event Helen Cameron has now decided to vacate the field.

I have concentrated on Helen Cameron as a prominent advocate of the pastoral cycle in this country, the field I know well, but before making comparisons with the four-source model, it is worth looking briefly at one other voice, or rather a polyphony, as gathered by Frans Wijsen and colleagues.

The Pastoral Circle Revisited (2005)

The *Pastoral Circle Revisited* is an assessment of the development of the pastoral circle over the 25 years since the publication of Joe Holland and Peter Henriot's *Social analysis: Linking Faith and Justice* (1980). An important contextual observation by the editors is the way in which the model is named (pastoral circle, spiral or cycle) in different parts of the world, with each term carrying different connotations. They observe that the term *pastoral cycle*

> ... is the more popular term in United Kingdom, Australia and Asia;
> ... seems more popular in pastoral care, pastoral theology, retreat pro-
> grams and religious education.
>
> (Wijsen, Henriot and Mejía, 2005, xxi)

To this researcher it is striking how frequently the 15 contributors to this collection assert both the importance of the presence of the researcher or activist in the stark reality of the situation or context being observed and the necessity of sharing with the reader the background of the researcher. For example, in the preface the celebrated liberation theologian Jon Sobrino talks of '"getting a grip" on reality which requires us *to be truly and actively involved in reality*, affected by things as they are; it is not sufficient to be intellectually face to face' (Wijsen, Henriot and Mejía, 2005, ix); Peter Henriot says that 'genuine contact with experience is essential'

(24); Juan José Luna insists that 'the first and second steps of the pastoral circle should not be done by someone coming from outside ... but people who are living in the situation' (38); and Maria Riley introduces herself in detail because 'social location is a critical element in the social analysis process' (184).

Juan José Luna precedes his remarks on outsiders by insisting how important it had been to train members of the CCJP (Catholic Commission for Justice and Peace); 'not by *teaching* but *training*' he emphasizes, showing the importance of the experiential nature of theological reflection as something that you do with the whole person rather than just think or speculate. This is reinforced by the experience of José de Mesa who, in stressing the importance of truth in the pastoral circle process, notes that there is 'no easy way to learning serious theological reflection', and that 'one needs to be trained in it' (104).

These convictions support my criticism of the way in which Helen Cameron's reflection groups were formed; as detailed above (see page 163), nothing is known about their background or ability to theologically reflect, especially in a group. This vindicates the co-operative inquiry groups in my research where the participants were already trained in the four-source model and came together to seek to improve its effectiveness, acting as their own insider facilitators.

Our concern that the pastoral cycle dominates the field is shared by Pete Ward in a recent publication:

> Given the range of methodological and theoretical debates in practical theology, it is quite surprising that when it comes to theological reflection as part of the curriculum, there is really only one method [*sic*] that is often taught: the pastoral cycle.
>
> (2017, 102)

We share his concerns that the pastoral cycle: 'tends to focus on occasions when there are problems in a pastoral context' (2017, 100), thereby missing the opportunity to explore moments of joy and celebration;[4] effectively has a step which is the theological step thereby making 'theology into one stage in a process' (102) rather than the whole model being theological; and that good theological reflection does not always have to 'start with experience' (113), but, as we have indicated, can start with Scripture, a position statement or something discerned in the culture we inhabit.

Comparing and contrasting the four-source model and pastoral cycle

Conversation

In *Talking about God in Practice* the second characteristic of this approach is the use of a framework of four voices of espoused, operant, formal and normative theology to create a conversational framework. This framework is seen as producing a language which can be used by 'practitioners, church leaders, and professional theologians' (Cameron et al., 2010, 147); this is commendable and I find this approach very useful in teaching. By contrast, the four-source model encourages not a conversation between those outside and inside a context; rather, between four sources which are *part* of that context: Experience, Tradition, Position and Culture. The best practice chapter above indicates the appropriate steps which may be taken in order to launch this theological conversation, but the way in which I have encouraged people to map the reflection, ideally on a wall, gives a visual presentation to the experienced reality, which is the conversation taking place between the four sources.

In contrast, the pastoral cycle tends to proceed by sequential steps with each one 'building upon the previous one' (Cameron, 2010, 9) and there is a sense of this being undertaken in a 'methodical way' (17). This discipline is employed in order to resist the temptation to 'jump to planning for the future' (Cameron et al., 2012, 81) rather than to engage in a more profound theological reflection or conversation. Jumping ahead is a natural response for some people and is common in ordinary conversation for which there are not usually any rules to order or control the conversation, unlike for example a formal debate, synod or parliament where rules or protocol may be adhered to. The four-source model with its combination of indicative steps combined with an emphasis on a model of conversation permits contributions which at first sight appear 'out of order'. In the Kelowna group's research cycle two a theological reflection began in the culture source on tipping.[5] In the planning session the agreed intention for the cycle was to undertake 'a theological reflection ... up to the generation of an image' (2013, 6). This means that the group is following steps 1–6 in the Culture column. The agreed account of the cycle records:

On the way several areas of tradition were noted:

- 'we are not worthy . . .' (Prayer of Humble Access)
- 'even the lilies of the field' (Matthew 6.28)
- Esther waiting for the King

(2013, 7)

Exploration of the tradition source will not take place until step 9, yet somewhere along the way during steps 1–6 several aspects of tradition are mentioned. The character of the four-source model as a conversation between sources allows these detours into the tradition, and the good practice of mapping the reflection meant that these three ideas were neither lost nor allowed to divert the group from its main task. When the group eventually got to step 6 they chose the passage about Queen Esther as the one they wanted to explore. In this way the model allows the practice of the art of theological reflection, following the discipline of a pathway and enabling conversation to move from source to source spontaneously.

Theological conversation

What makes a conversation or reflection theological?

In their own way each of the three major ambassadors for the pastoral cycle in the United Kingdom names theology as a *stage* in the reflection: Laurie Green names it as the third stage, after experience and exploration, when the 'process of theological reflection brings things into even clearer perspective' (1990, 75); Paul Ballard and John Pritchard also name it as the third stage of the pastoral cycle (1996, 17); and Helen Cameron's concern about the jump to planning is because this inevitably skips the 'theological step', engaging with the Christian tradition (Cameron et al., 2012, 81). This approach whereby the engagement with Scripture or tradition is seen as something that takes place after analysis is understandable given the model's roots as a tool for social and political change. In the updated version of their 1980 work Joe Holland and Peter Henriot, in adding an afterword, offer a framework for theological reflection, insisting that in the pastoral circle social analysis and theological reflection are 'closely related' (1983, 103). Again, given this heritage, it is no surprise that even though the pastoral cycle is now regarded by many as a model of theological reflection, the theological element is still seen as an identifiable step.

By contrast, I would claim that the four-source model does not have a separate or discrete theological step, but is a conversation between sources, one of which is the Christian tradition, such that when all the sources are present in the conversation, then it is a theological conversation. It is not simply the Christian tradition which makes it theological, but the confluence of all four sources.

Position

None of the co-operative inquiry groups expressed any concerns about making connections with the Christian tradition, but is there a possibility that denomination is a factor in the environment in which theological reflection takes place? The issue is mentioned several times in Cameron's work where the relationship between personal experience and the Christian tradition is described as a 'tension' (Cameron et al., 2010, 25) in a work which is proud of its ecumenical make-up (22), and if she sees theological reflection as undertaken through the 'lens' (14) of tradition, to what extent is the reflection constrained by that tradition? When she draws upon the work of John Reader (2005) in exploring 'blurred encounters' (pastoral situations on the edge of one's theological faith position) there is the possibility that a person may have their faith compromised (Cameron et al., 2012, 17). In what may be a simple case of serendipity she uses the phrase 'faith position', resonating with the use of that term for a source in the four-source model. The strength of the four-source model in identifying Position as a source is that it gives a person a language and a tool to help discern what is happening in their internal processes. For example, I may be feeling uncomfortable at this moment in the theological reflection because we are touching on an issue which clashes with a position I hold. The identification of my position in a reflection may give an individual space to reconsider their position vis-à-vis their denomination's position. In reverse, the four-source understanding of Position resonates with Cameron's use of the 'four voices of theology' where normative theology is the official church teaching (2010, 54). Our model of theological reflection, which gives a voice to four different sources, is not the same as Patricia Killen and John de Beer's, where 'theological reflection involves bringing religious heritage ... into our reflection on experience' (1994, 52). For them the four sources of their model – Action, Positions, Culture and Tradition – are 'aspects of Experience' (59). Is this approach affected by their denominational adherence, and particularly Patricia Killen's, as a Roman Catholic, that the religious heritage takes such a dominant part? Patricia has generously confirmed that 20 years later she stands by this original claim for theological reflection being a conversation between experience and the religious heritage: 'I want to emphasize that a model of sources is not a model of theological reflection.'[6]

Culture

Helen Cameron uses a definition of culture which is attractive in its simplicity. Culture includes 'the objects, shapes, texts and images that surround us' (Cameron et al., 2010, 21). She derives this definition from the work of Kathryn Tanner. However, a weakness of this approach, and of the pastoral cycle, is that it is not clear what the relationship between culture and theology is. Elsewhere the relationship appears to be one of enmity: culture is 'resistant to religion' (Cameron et al., 2010, 9); practices of faith have to rescued from the 'clutches of ... cultural forces' (13); and culture is a 'vexed question' (21). By overtly naming culture as a source, the four-source module of theological reflection addresses culture head on, gives culture a voice at the table, and freed from denominational constraints allows the practitioner to weigh for themselves the extent to which the cultural voice will be heard.

The centring of the four-source model around an image encourages the imagination, and the valuing of culture as a source encourages a sense of diversity that culture brings rather than defensiveness or fear – it encourages consideration of both context and imagination. There is some acknowledgement of the power of culture when Helen Cameron is considering the difficulties her action learning event had in dealing with the Bible:

> ... in the light of Gadamer's work we can no longer think that any interpretation is free of cultural prejudice (Gadamer, 2004). We have to face up to the fact that ... we are all contextual theologians now.
>
> (Cameron et al., 2012, 88)

This struggle appears to come out of a sense of frustration that the action learning event could not come up with any definitive approach to tradition and therefore no specific answers to the issues being explored. Is this naive? Kathryn Tanner says that a postmodern cultural approach values diversity and sees this as leading to a theological creativity characterized not by a lack of shape or clear voice, but rather by a 'bricoleur' of voices, colours and nuances (1997, 166).

Comparing and contrasting the four-source model and 'four voices in theology'

As companions on the Way (Acts 24.14) with Helen Cameron and her colleagues, I welcome their exposition of a model of four voices in theology. These are:

- the *operant* theology of a group or community which is manifest in its day-to-day practice;
- the *normative* voice of theology which is heard through the scriptures, creeds, liturgies and teachings of the Church;

- the *espoused* theology which is revealed in the way in which a community or group articulates its belief – what it *says* it believes;
- and *formal* theology which is the theology of theologians – what is sometimes called the academy.

(2010, 54)

The four voices in theology and four-source module of reflection are trying to achieve similar outcomes. They both provide a model by which theology may be explored and refined by believers who are seeking understanding, and both attempt to provide a language – albeit imperfect – to begin to talk about the God we experience; talking about God in practice. They do not map one on top of the other but they do connect in several ways.

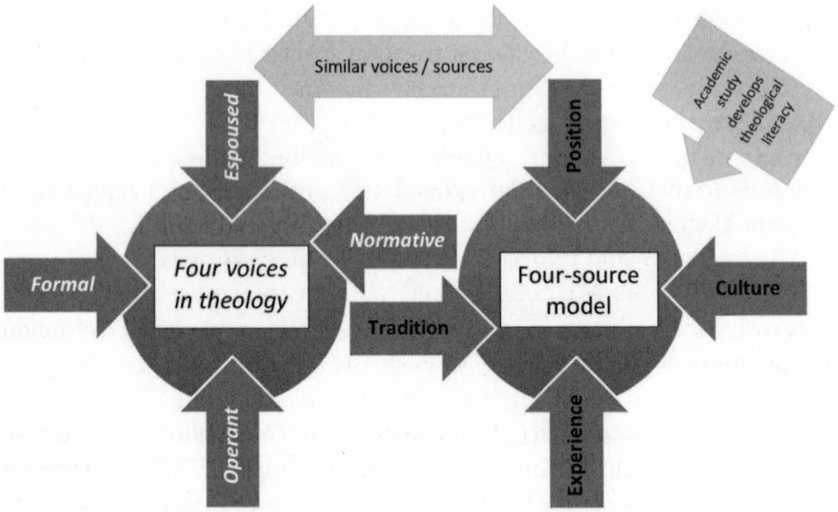

Figure 21 Four voices and four sources

As indicated in Figure 21, the two models share a common source, Tradition, by which I mean our heritage of the Judeo–Christian tradition of several thousand years, and the voices in theology model describes the normative voice, found in the Scriptures, creeds, liturgies and teachings of the Church. I would argue that there is also a second similar source or voice in that a person's espoused theology may in fact be an expression of a person's position in the four-source model. The use of the concept of Position in the four-source model might help practitioners using the voice in theology module to tease out for themselves the difference between their espoused and operant theologies. In the voices in theology model the field of academic theology is named as a voice; in the four-source model, as practitioners, we recognize the value of continued academic study and how this underpins any process of theological reflection.

However, perhaps a more fruitful way of comparing and using the two models is that the four-source model of theological reflection is one way in which a person may explore their operant theology. A continued and disciplined use of the four-source model means that an individual or group is constantly exploring the way in which four sources – Experience, Culture, Tradition and Position – shape a person's theology; that is, what weight does a person invest in each of the different sources and does this weighting change when exploring different aspects of life?

Theological integrity in a person deepens when the distance between espoused and operant theology is narrowed and eventually removed. A life lived in the four-source model is a life in which both experience and culture are taken seriously and welcomed at the table of critical theological conversation.

Models of theological reflection in dialogue

The four-source model is not offered as a replacement to the pastoral cycle, neither is it simply another form of the pastoral cycle.

As a developed and published model of theological reflection the four-source model stands as a critical friend to the pastoral cycle and vice versa. In a conversation between the two models the four-source model might ask practitioners of the pastoral cycle questions such as:

- How can you be confident that the prejudices and beliefs (Position) of the practitioner are not unduly directing the outcome of the reflection?
- How can you demonstrate that the choice of Scripture called upon by the practitioner is not being used as a proof text?
- In what way is the operant theology of the practitioner shaped by the cultural context?
- Is the practitioner clinging too closely to the operant theology of her tradition rather than considering the possibility of letting it go?
- Why are you so obsessed with a practical outcome – is not a developed theology a practical outcome?
- What happens if you risk taking the steps of the models in a different order?
- What about pursuing side loops (which may themselves spiral) as well as generating spirals?

And in the conversation the pastoral cycle might ask practitioners of the four-source model questions such as:

- Is your reflection rooted in a detailed analysis of the context in which you are exploring?
- Are you aware of different theologies (operant, espoused, etc.) at play in the people involved in the theological reflection?

Even when the operant theologies of participants or researchers are identified it is not always clear what should happen to them. The four-source model understanding of Position encourages it to be declared. So when Cameron and her colleagues worry about how 'members of the outside team deal with the fact they have greater empathy with ...' (Cameron et al., 2010, 73), a recognition of this as a 'position' would liberate all concerned. This is consistent with the concluding sentiments of Frans Wijsen and colleagues in their survey of the pastoral circle landscape: they ask, 'What are the dispositions that we bring as we enter into the pastoral circle process?' (Disposition is acknowledged in the four-source model as Position.) They also acknowledge 'the need to recognize implicit theology', which is seen in Cameron's work as operant theology (Wijsen, Henriot and Mejía, 2005, 227).

The robustness of the models

The pastoral cycle and the field of action research share the foundational principle that reflection should lead to action. The liberation theology movement of Latin America, with its use of the 'see, judge, act' model, is often trumpeted as the parent of the pastoral cycle. Joe Holland claims that the historical roots of the model are in fact even deeper, reaching back through nearly 300 years of papal encyclicals (which follow a similar pattern) to the appropriation in Paris during the thirteenth century by Thomas Aquinas of the African Islamic Aristotelian tradition of southern Spain (Wijsen, Henriot and Mejía, 2005, 10). In this long heritage the importance of action is self-evident.

In action research the validity criteria offered by Herr and Anderson has 'achievement of action-orientated outcomes' as the second of five goals (2005, 54). In the co-operative inquiry groups, the principles and methods of the four-source model were used to research the four-source model. While this might appear collusive or generative of a circular argument, it does in fact affirm the robustness of the model and its capacity to produce practical outcomes. By robustness I mean that the model has depth, or breadth or, more colloquially, 'has legs'. The research cycles never dried up because there was always more to explore – each group had insufficient time to run down all the research questions posed by the different cycles. The model was capable of exploring issues as wide as the social mores of tipping (Kelowna, 2013, 6); the politics of healthcare (Auckland, 2013, 10); exploring how to sell a product – E*f*M Australia – (Brisbane, 2013, 5); and contemporary art (Sewanee, 2013, 5).

By contrast, the action outcomes identified by Cameron in her work do appear limited. An action learning event was derailed over the issue of the use of Scripture (see page 162) and the number of cycles ARCS research projects undertake is limited (see page 158). In *Talking about God in Practice* it is interesting to note that of the five characteristics that Cameron et al. identify for theological action research, none is an overtly action outcome; the emphasis is on theological language and forming practice theologically (2010, 145–51).

In *Theological Reflection for Human Flourishing* Helen Cameron concludes that the third challenge the research has thrown up is 'to ask if the model of the pastoral cycle has been stretched too far beyond its normal purposes' (2012, 119). By contrast, there is a tendency in the literature on theological reflection for the Killen and de Beer model to be pigeonholed into a personal wisdom category. For example, Robert Kinast (2000) identifies seven different styles of theological reflection and places *the art of theological reflection* in the Spiritual Wisdom style chapter.[7] Judith Thompson and colleagues place the model under a section called 'Reflections for Imagination and Spiritual Wisdom' (Thompson, Pattison and Thompson, 2008, 65). Laurie Green in preparing the new edition of his book includes the work of Patricia Killen and John de Beer and puts it under a section named 'The personal walk with God' (Green, 2009, 139).

Part of my argument and the experience of the co-operative inquiry groups is that the four-source model, as we have developed it, is a rich and robust process of theological reflection. One way to develop best practice in the four-source model is to take aspects of good practice from other recognized models.

The four-source model can be adapted at step 3 in the reflection beginning from the culture source or from experience to include more detailed social analysis as reflected by Wijsen and colleagues (Wijsen, Henriot and Mejía, 2005) (see page 42). This would give greater credence to the four-source model as one that is sociologically embedded – a tool for individuals and communities to use to help make sense of the complex world in which we live, rather than merely one for personal spiritual devolvement. In a similar way, a detailed exegesis of the text in the method from tradition source at step 3 (see page 42) might be conducted (for the other methods at step 9, see page 43, could be encouraged), again adding integrity to the model.

Conclusion

In focusing on Helen Cameron, we do not seek to suggest that the pastoral cycle per se cannot be used in action research; rather, the way in which it is predominantly used in the United Kingdom is a pale shadow of its use in other parts of the world.

For Wijsen et al. the pastoral circle is understood by those who use it to be a tool for cultivating *action*, and the strong emphasis on being *in* the action implies that the way they instinctively practise the pastoral circle *is* a form of action research (though they would not use that term) because they do it *with* people whereas Cameron is essentially qualitative. There is a continuum here whereby Wijsen and colleagues working primarily in the majority world, use the pastoral circle as a means to social *action* and from that stance view the West (the minority world) as using the pastoral cycle for 'softer' contexts – that is, for theological *insight*; Cameron et al. see the four-source model as presented to them via Killen and de Beer as looking for *spiritual* insight. This book argues that the four-source model is in fact more robust than the pastoral cycle in producing action, theological insight and theological training, and may be seen as a kind of 'continuing ministerial development'[8] where 'minister' includes every Christian person, since all are ministers by virtue of their baptism. This is exemplified by the experience of a participant in the Brisbane group,[9] who despite years of ministerial practice found the reflection process to be forming him still.

The pastoral cycle is in danger of ignoring its radical heritage, becoming another tool with which to do research *on* people rather than *with* people. The four-source model is perceived as not being action oriented, so a greater emphasis on the kind of social analysis (see page 164) encouraged by the pastoral circle would give a stronger indication that practitioners of the model are engaged in practical reflection leading to action.

The emergence of a stronger school of practitioners grounded in the four-source model might encourage a mutual recognition leading to mutual enrichment.

As a contribution to practical theology, I believe that a co-operative inquiry group using the four-source model of theological reflection to shape the reflexive life of researchers is exemplary because of the values contained in such an approach. Co-operative inquiry ensures that research is undertaken *with* people, thus acknowledging and respecting our co-dependency on God who creates and sustains. Employing the four-source model in reflexivity ensures that each person's experience is taken seriously, roots our work in our Judeo-Christian heritage, welcomes culture as a conversation partner, and actively encourages the sharing and challenging of personal or theological positions which are grist to the mill of creative, informed critical theological conversation. I commend it to you.

Notes

1 Killen and de Beer (1994, 87–110), Cameron's footnote.

2 See page 19 – the italics in the Bradbury and Reason quotation indicate their emphasis, not mine.

3 The experiential nature of the event is only acknowledged at the end of the book (2012, 119).

4 There are exceptions. Heather Warren and her colleagues are unusual in recognizing that theological reflection is not just something you do when you have a problem, but a discipline for daily life, including times of distress and crisis, and also times of celebration (Warren, Murray and Best, 2002).

5 In this country we would probably talk about leaving a tip or gratuity.

6 Patricia O'Connell Killen, email message to author, 2 May 2014.

7 To be fair to him he does at the end of his chapter note that the authors affirm the practical outcome of their reflection style, but again in noting that the method *may* prompt persons to action, rather than *will* lead to action, the reader might infer that Patricia Killen and John de Beer's approach to reflection would lead to action only *occasionally*.

8 CMD is a term used by some Anglicans for the on-going learning of clergy.

9 See the Brisbane account (2013, 16).

12

Final thoughts

GARY O'NEILL

As practitioners we do our best to instil the idea that the four-source model is essentially a conversation between four sources; however, in practice we recognize that some people get hung up on the number or order of the steps, effectively beginning to lose sight of the wood for the trees (you will have already guessed that we are fond of using images!). In Chapter 4 we talked about developing facilitation skills as being like taking time to look under the bonnet of the car which you are already happy driving and in Chapter 3 used the analogy of learning to swim, drive or ride a bicycle. In my experience most people do not claim to have acquired any of these skills by simply jumping into a pool to swim four lengths, or hopping on to a bicycle for a mile, or legally driving a car without either considerable practice and, probably, in some cases, considerable instruction or coaching.

Interestingly, the older we are the longer it takes to acquire the skills for swimming, cycling or driving – if you are unsure of that try asking a friend or colleague who learned to swim as an adult. To date we have spent most of our time helping adults learn the skills of theological reflection, although one of our colleagues, Beverley Angier, has used the model with teenagers very successfully.

The point about this illustration is that there comes a time for each person when they can swim, ride a bike or drive a car without assistance and then something remarkable happens – after a while we no longer think about how to do it. Sometimes one of the biggest obstacles to adults learning is the fear of failure or embarrassment, and so part of our self declares that we cannot do whatever it is we are learning: it is not my learning style; I do not think like that; I am a scientist (or literary person); and the classic, I do not think in images, theological reflection for me is like pulling teeth!

Nearly 30 years ago, the theological adult educator John Hull, in the preface to the American edition of his work, reaffirmed his conviction that there is 'an implicit set of values within much orthodox Christian theology which has the effect of lowering an expectation that change and growth will take place' (Hull, 1991). When this cultural context is added to the individual reluctance in some adults to learn, combined with a twenty-first-century consumerism which desires a quick fix, the scale of the task we face in developing learning environments becomes considerable.

Theological reflection groups are one way in which to provide a safe learning space. They are a place where those nurturing the preaching life envisioned by Liz will be nourished. They are home to poets like Andrew and will flourish under the caring oversight of parish priests such as Robin. What all of these who have contributed to this book have in common is a desire – a thirst welling up – and longing to enjoy what Judith describes as an ethos or way of life. For me it is a *habitus*.[1]

One of the highlights for me of the research in the international co-operative inquiry groups is tucked away in the agreed account of the Brisbane group. At the end of the conference when the group were using Kathryn Herr and Gary Anderson's validity criteria as a way to evaluate the event (2005, 55), under a section about the learning of participants, the account simply records:

One mentor said that he was becoming a four-source person.

(Brisbane, 2013, 17)

What this says to me is that the person was in the process of acquiring a new habitus. This is a discipline for daily life, for use in the ordinary and the extraordinary. The person engaged in theological reflection seeks not only to grasp truth more deeply, but to be more deeply grasped by the truth (Warren, Murray and Best, 2002). Becoming a four-source person is a new *habitus*.

We do not claim that the four-source model is going to be useful for everyone, but we do recognize that it is a skill which many find takes a long time to acquire before they have the revelatory 'aha' or 'light bulb' moment. Like swimming, cycling or driving it can take time. We believe it is well worth the personal investment of time and resources.

A couple of parables

As we have indicated by our exploration of biblical study, preaching and poetry, insightful theological reflection demands the use of the imagination, the ability to let oneself go, to see what it is like, as Andrew reminded us, to be someone or something else.

Imagine this

The prophet Nathan, appalled by the behaviour of the king, wonders whether a new cure he has heard of might bring the sovereign to his senses. The new cure implies that the simple act of publicly telling the king his actions are immoral before applying a solution of social analysis regarding the palace's drain on the populace and the country, followed by a second ladle of significant texts from the Scriptures, can lead to a new dawn in which everything changes and the king asks to be told more. The prophet hesitates and recalls the king's prodigious intellectual capacity for mental gymnastics. He breaks his fast with the king the next day and tells him a story: 'There were two men in a certain city, one rich ... the poor man had nothing but one little ewe lamb.'[2]

Finally

I am inspired by Terry Veling's (2005, 69) quote of Ellen Charry's description of Aquinas at work.

> One imagines his study filled with books. As Thomas writes (or dictates) each article of the Summa one can see scripture at his right hand, Augustine's great corpus at his left, Aristotle's philosophy on a table nearby, the works of the Fathers piled up on the floor, and the questions and perplexities of the monks he taught and lived with written on scraps of parchment and arranged in the order of topics as he would tackle them. One sees secretaries scurrying to find the precise wording of the citations he has requested, and copyists awaiting the finished manuscript. And one can hear the clucking of those who criticized the new synthesis of truth and knowledge as it appeared.
>
> (Charry, 1997, 185–6)

Our ability as human beings both to describe the world we inhabit and, for the reader, to imagine someone else's world through their words is one of the reasons why the use of generated images in theological reflection is so powerful. So to paraphrase Ellen Charry, I see myself writing in a small study surrounded by textbooks and novels. As I write the earlier drafts of this book (having given up on *Dragon Naturally Speaking*) I have: my *annotated story* at my right hand; Bradbury and Reason's *Handbook of Action Research* at my left; Bonnie Miller-McLemore's *Wiley-Blackwell Companion to Practical Theology* on a table nearby; a stack of John Heron and Peter Reason's books on the floor; and a flow of emails from colleagues and students ranging from one who cannot find a file on their computer to another concerned about the imminent effect of treatment for cancer on their ministerial prospects. The supportive publisher wishes I would get on and complete, while others are suspicious of this 'new kid on the block' researcher – combining classical theology with humanist action research – whatever next! The dog wants to go out again and deftly sidesteps the tower of adult education books by the door, unwisely topped off by my ridiculously heavy copy of *Handbook of Adult and Continuing Education* (Wilson, Hayes and Education, 2000). And where did I leave my journal (annotated copy)?

My dream is that my annotated copy be replaced by this book and that this book finds a home in others' studies or living rooms.

Notes

1 Acknowledging the work of Edward Farley (1983), Elaine Graham and her colleagues define *habitus* as 'a disposition of the mind and heart from which our actions flow naturally' (Graham, Walton and Ward, 2007).

2 2 Samuel 12.1–13, where David repents after hearing the story of the poor man and his stolen lamb.

Glossary

Terms in brackets are for information; their use is discouraged.

A reflection starting from an experience	A reflection rooted in an individual's experience and shared with the group.
A reflection starting from shared experience	A reflection rooted in an experience which is common to everyone in the group, e.g. waking up this morning.
Conversation	The relationship between the four sources is akin to a conversation.
Experience	What happened.
Faith stories	A description of how God has worked in a person's life.
Heart of the matter	The distillation of a source into a single word or phrase.
Image	The heart of the matter of a source translated into a picture or world that can be imagined.
Interrogatory	The name given to questions used to explore an image, source or world – they are rooted in doctrinal/theological concepts.
Knack	A skill gained through experience.
Orientation	The process of exploring a world – having a look around.

Standpoint	The place from which an image is examined, e.g. the place where you are standing.
Thought shower	A more positive and imaginative expression than brain storm.
What is the world like?	In best practice the question is about orientation – it can also be used as an interrogatory question rooted in Creation.
World	The imagined place, situation or context which an image evokes in the imagination.
[Action]	The E*f*M and Killen and de Beer term for Experience.
[Correlation]	One way of describing the relationship between two sources; our preference is for *conversation*.
[Explore]	How Killen and de Beer describe linking the heart of the matter with the Christian heritage.
[Metaphor]	The E*f*M term for image.
[Microscope method]	The E*f*M term used to denote a reflection rooted in an individual's experience.
[Perspective]	The E*f*M term used to describe an interrogatory question.
[Spiritual autobiographies]	The E*f*M term for faith stories.
[Wide angle method]	The E*f*M term for a reflection rooted in a broad theme.

Bibliography

Agnew, Jonathan (2010, Sunday 28 November), 'I love winding up Geoffrey Boy-cott', *The Observer*, www.guardian.co.uk/theobserver/2010/nov/28/jonathan -agnew-ashes-cricket-interview.

Alexander, Elizabeth (2006), 'Ars Poetica #100: I Believe', *American Blue: Selected Poems*, Tarset: Bloodaxe.

Astley, Jeff (2002), *Ordinary Theology: Looking, Listening and Learning in The-ology*, Aldershot: Ashgate.

Astley, Jeff and Francis, Leslie J. (2013), *Exploring Ordinary Theology: Everyday Christian Believing and the Church*, Farnham, Surrey, UK; Burlington, VT: Ash-gate.

Auckland (2013), Account of the Auckland co-operative inquiry group, www. dropbox.com/sh/h3zqv6zzteybo1i/AACom9F48QvSKoryhpiaAeu4a/Auckland. pdf?dl=0.

Aymer, Cathy (2001), 'Researching the experiences of black professionals in white organisations', in Richard Winter and Carol Munn-Giddings (eds), *A Handbook for Action Research in Health and Social Care* (pp. 131–44), London; New York: Routledge.

Ballard, Paul H. (2012), 'The use of scripture', in Bonnie J. Miller-McLemore and Wiley-Blackwell (Firm) (eds), *The Wiley-Blackwell Companion to Practical The-ology* (pp. 163–72), Malden, MA: Wiley-Blackwell.

Ballard, Paul H. and Pritchard, John (1996), *Practical Theology in Action: Christian Thinking in the Service of Church and Society*, London: SPCK.

Ballard, Paul H. and Pritchard, John (2006), *Practical Theology in Action: Christian Thinking in the Service of Church and Society* (2nd edn), London: SPCK.

Barth, Karl (1968), *The Epistle to the Romans* (Vol. 261), Oxford: Oxford Uni-versity Press.

Bergland, James W. (1969), 'Field education as locus for theological reflection', *Theological Education*, 5(4) (pp. 338–45).

Bevans, Stephen B. (1992), *Models of Contextual Theology*, Maryknoll, NY: Orbis Books.

Blake, W. (1972), *Complete Writings: With Variant Readings*, vol. 190, Oxford; New York: Oxford University Press.

Bolton, Gillie (2010), *Reflective Practice: Writing and Professional Development* (3rd edn), London: Sage.

Borg, M. J. (2011), *Speaking Christian: Recovering the Lost Meaning of Christian Words*, London: SPCK.

Brisbane (2013), Account of the Brisbane co-operative inquiry group, www.dropbox. com/s/vw61050pad20cch/Brisbane.pdf.

Brown, Frank Burch (1982), 'Transfiguration: poetic metaphor and theological reflection', *The Journal of Religion*, 62(1) (pp. 39–56).

Brown, Raymond E. (1975), *Biblical Reflections on Crises Facing the Church*, London: Darton, Longman and Todd.

Brown, Raymond E., Murphy, Roland E. and Fitzmyer, Joseph A. (1968), *The Jerome Biblical Commentary*, London: G. Chapman.

Brown, Teresa L. Fry (2003), *Weary Throats and New Songs: Black Women Proclaiming God's Word*, Nashville, TN: Abingdon Press.

Brueggemann, Walter (1978), *The Prophetic Imagination*, Philadelphia, PA: Fortress Press.

Brueggemann, Walter (1986), *Hopeful Imagination: Prophetic Voices in Exile*, Philadelphia, PA: Fortress Press.

Brueggemann, Walter (1997), *Cadences of Home: Preaching Among Exiles* (1st edn), Louisville, KY: Westminster John Knox Press.

Brueggemann, Walter (2012), *The Practice of Prophetic Imagination*, Minneapolis, MN: Fortress Press.

Buber, Martin (2008), *I and Thou*, New York: Simon & Schuster.

Burns, Danny (2007), *Systemic Action Research: A Strategy for Whole System Change*, Bristol: Policy Press.

Caffarella, Rosemary and Meriam, Sharan B. (2000), 'Linking the individual learner to the context of adult learning', in Arthur L. Wilson, Elisabeth Hayes, and American Association for Adult and Continuing Education (eds), *Handbook of Adult Continuing Education* (pp. 55–70), San Francisco, CA: Jossey-Bass.

Cameron, Helen (2010), *Resourcing Mission*, London: SCM Press.

Cameron, Helen (2015), *Just Mission: Practical Politics for Local Churches*, London: SCM Press.

Cameron, Helen, Bhatti, Deborah, Duce, Catherine, Sweeney, James and Watkins, Clare (2010), *Talking about God in Practice: Theological Action Research and Practical Theology*, London: SCM Press.

Cameron, Helen and Duce, Catherine (2013), *Researching Practice in Mission and Ministry: A Companion*, London: SCM Press.

Cameron, Helen, Reader, John, Slater, Victoria and Rowland, Chris (2012), *Theological Reflection for Human Flourishing: Pastoral Practice and Public Theology*, London: SCM Press.

Chambers, Robert (2002), *Participatory Workshops: A Sourcebook of 21 Sets of Ideas and Activities*, London: Earthscan.

Charry, Ellen T. (1997), *By the Renewing of Your Minds: The Pastoral Function of Christian Doctrine*, New York; Oxford: Oxford University Press.

Chiu, Lai Fong (2008), 'Health promotion and participatory action research: the significance of participatory praxis in developing participatory health intervention', in *The SAGE Handbook of Action Research: Participative Inquiry and Practice* (pp. 534–49), Los Angeles, CA; London; New Delhi; Singapore: Sage.

Coghlan, David (2005), 'Ignatian spirituality as transformational social science', *Action Research*, 3(1) (pp. 89–107).

Coghlan, David and Brannick, Teresa (2014), *Doing Action Research in Your Own Organization* (4th edn), London: Sage.

Comstock, W. Richard (1968), 'Marshall McLuhan's theory of sensory form: a theological reflection', *Soundings: An Interdisciplinary Journal*, 51(2) (pp. 166–83).

Conde-Frazier, Elizabeth (2012), 'Participatory action research', in Bonnie J. Miller-McLemore (ed.), *The Wiley-Blackwell Companion to Practical Theology* (pp. 234–43), Malden, MA; Oxford: Wiley-Blackwell.

Copeland, Jennifer Elaine (2014), *Feminine Registers: The Importance of Women's Voices for Christian Preaching*, Eugene, OR: Cascade Books.

Darragh, Neil (1995), *Doing Theology Ourselves: A Guide to Research and Action*, Cardiff: Accent.

de Bary, Edward O. (1994), 'A history of the Education for Ministry program: 1975–1992', *Sewanee Theological Review*, 37(3) (pp. 227–61).

de Bary, Edward O. (2003), *Theological Reflection: The Creation of Spiritual Power in the Information Age*, Collegeville, MN: Liturgical Press.

Dix, Dom Gregory (1945), *The Shape of the Liturgy*, London: Dacre Press.

Dulles, Avery (1976), 'Review of David Tracy's *Blessed Rage for Order*', *Theological Studies*, 37 (pp. 307–09).

Education for Ministry (2013), *Reading and Reflection Guide*, Vol. A, Richard E. Brewer (ed.).

Ellison, Pat Taylor and Keifert, Patrick R. (2011), *Dwelling in the Word: A Pocket Handbook*, Robbinsdale, MN: Church Innovations.

Farley, Edward (1983), *Theologia: The Fragmentation and Unity of Theological Education*, Philadelphia, PA: Fortress Press.

Freire, Paulo (1972), *Pedagogy of the Oppressed*, Myra Bergman Ramos (trans), Harmondsworth: Penguin.

Frost, Michael (2006), *Exiles: Living Missionally in a Post-Christian Culture*, Peabody, MA: Hendrickson Publishers.

Fulkerson, Mary McClintock (2007), *Places of Redemption: Theology for a Worldly Church*, Oxford; New York: Oxford University Press.

Gadamer, Hans-Georg (2004), *Truth and Method*, London: Continuum.

Ganzevoort, R. Ruard (2009), 'Forks in the Road when Tracing the Sacred. Practical Theology as Hermeneutics of Lived Religion', paper presented at the International Academy of Practical Theology, Chicago, IL.

Gibson, Owen (2011, 25 January, retrieved 26 February 2013, www.guardian. co.uk/football/2011/jan/25/andy-gray-sacked-sky), Andy Gray sacked by Sky for 'unacceptable and offensive behaviour'.

Graham, Elaine (2013), 'Is practical theology a form of "action research"?', *International Journal of Practical Theology*, 17(1) (p. 148).

Graham, Elaine, Walton, Heather and Ward, Frances (2005), *Theological Reflection: Methods*, London: SCM Press.

Graham, Elaine, Walton, Heather and Ward, Frances (2007), *Theological Reflection: Sources*, London: SCM Press.

Green, Laurie (1990), *Let's Do Theology: A Pastoral Cycle Resource Book*, London: Continuum.

Green, Laurie (2009), *Let's Do Theology*, London: Mowbray.

Greenwood, Davydd J. and Levin, Morten (2007), *Introduction to Action Research: Social Research for Social Change* (2nd edn), Thousand Oaks, CA: Sage.

Guhathakurta, Meghna (2008), 'Theatre in participatory action research: Experiences from Bangladesh', in Peter Reason and Hilary Bradbury (eds), *The SAGE Handbook of Action Research: Participative Inquiry and Practice* (pp. 510–21), Los Angeles, CA; London; New Delhi; Singapore: Sage.

Gunner, Susanna (2013), 'Integrating ritual: an exploration of women's response to *woman-cross*', in Nicola Slee, Fran Porter and Anne Phillips (eds), *The Faith Lives of Women and Girls: Qualitative Research Perspectives*, Farnham: UK: Ashgate.

Heron, John (1989), *The Facilitators' Handbook*, London: Kogan Page.

Heron, John (1996), *Co-operative Inquiry: Research into the Human Condition*, London: Sage.

Heron, John (1999), *The Complete Facilitator's Handbook*, London: Kogan Page.

Heron, John and Lahood, Gregg (2008), 'Charismatic inquiry in concert: action research in the realm of "the between"', in Peter Reason and Hilary Bradbury (eds), *The SAGE Handbook of Action Research: Participative Inquiry and Practice* (2nd edn, pp. 439–62), Los Angeles, CA; London; New Delhi; Singapore: Sage.

Heron, John and Reason, Peter (2008), 'Extending epistemology within a co-operative inquiry', in Peter Reason and Hilary Bradbury (eds), *The SAGE Handbook of Action Research: Participative Inquiry and Practice* (pp. 366–80), Los Angeles, CA; London; New Delhi; Singapore: Sage.

Herr, Kathryn and Anderson, Gary L. (2005), *The Action Research Dissertation: A Guide for Students and Faculty*, London: Sage.

Hodgson, Peter Crafts and King, Robert Harlen (2008), *Christian Theology: An Introduction to its Traditions and Tasks* (3rd edn), London: SPCK.

Holland, Joe and Henriot, Peter (1980), *Social Analysis: Linking Faith and Justice*, Washington DC: Center of Concern.

Holland, Joe and Henriot, Peter (1983), *Social Analysis: Linking Faith and Justice* (rev. and enl. edn), Maryknoll, NY: Orbis Books in collaboration with the Center of Concern.

Hopkins, Gerard Manley (1986), 'God's Grandeur', in *Gerard Manley Hopkins: The Oxford Authors* (p. 128), Oxford: Oxford University Press.

Hull, John M. (1991), *What Prevents Christian Adults from Learning?* Philadelphia, PA: Trinity Press International.

Hull, John M. (2001), *In the Beginning there was Darkness: A Blind Person's Conversations with the Bible*, London: SCM Press.

Jasper, David (1989), *The Study of Literature and Religion: An Introduction* (p. 6), Basingstoke: Palgrave Macmillan.

Jenkins, David (1971a), 'Concerning theological reflection', *Study Encounter*, 7(3) (pp. 1–7).

Jenkins, David (1971b), *Human Rights from a Theological Perpsective*. Notes prepared for the CCIA Executive Committee, July 1971.

Jenkins, David O. (2017), 'Sanctifying grace in the integrating work of contextual education', in Kathleen A. Cahalan, Edward Foley and Gordon S. Mikoski (eds), *Integrating Work in Theological Education* (p. 109), Eugene, OR: Wipf & Stock Publishers.

Keller, Timothy and Keller, Kathy (2011), *The Meaning of Marriage: Facing the Complexities of Commitment with the Wisdom of God*, London: Hodder & Stoughton.

Kelowna (2013), Account of the Kelowna co-operative inquiry group, www.drop box.com/s/4da18ftskm61pcf/Kelowna.pdf.

Kemmis, Stephen (2008), 'Critical theory and participatory action research', in Peter Reason and Hilary Bradbury (eds), *The SAGE Handbook of Action Research: Participative Inquiry and Practice* (2nd edn, pp. 121–38), Los Angeles, CA; London; New Delhi; Singapore: Sage.

Killen, Patricia O'Connell (1995), 'Assisting adults to think theologically', in James D. Whitehead and Evelyn Eaton Whitehead (eds), *Method in Ministry:*

Theological Reflection and Christian Ministry (revd edn, pp. 103–10), Lanham, MD; New York; Oxford: Sheed & Ward.

Killen, Patricia O'Connell and de Beer, John (1983), '"Everyday" theology: a model for religious and theological education', *Chicago Studies*, 22(2) (p. 16).

Killen, Patricia O'Connell and de Beer, John (1994), *The Art of Theological Reflection*, New York: Crossroad.

Kinast, Robert L. (2000), *What Are They Saying about Theological Reflection?* New York: Paulist Press.

Knowles, Malcolm S. (1980), *The Modern Practice of Adult Education: From Pedagogy to Andragogy* (revd and updated edn), Wilton, Conn. Chicago: Association Press, Follett Pub. Co.

Knowles, S. (2011), 'Postmodernism: Reasons to be cheerful', in Hannah Bacon, Wayne Morris and Steve Knowles, *Transforming Exclusion: Engaging Faith Perspectives* (pp. 1–23), London: Continuum.

Kolb, David A. (1984), *Experiential Learning: Experience as the Source of Learning and Development*, Englewood Cliffs, NJ; London: Prentice-Hall.

Koshy, Valsa (2010), *Action Research for Improving Educational Practice: A Step-by-step Guide* (2nd edn), London: Sage.

Kuniholm, Whitney T. (2010), *Essential 100: Your Journey Through the Bible in 100 Readings*, Bletchley: Scripture Union.

Lakoff, George and Johnson, Mark (2003), *Metaphors We Live By*, Chicago: University of Chicago Press.

Levin, Morten (2008), 'The praxis of educating action researchers', in Peter Reason and Hilary Bradbury (eds), *The SAGE Handbook of Action Research: Participative Inquiry and Practice* (2nd edn, pp. 669–81), Los Angeles, CA; London: Sage.

Lonergan, Bernard J. F. (1972), *Method in Theology*, London: Darton, Longman and Todd.

Long, Thomas G. (1988), *The Senses of Preaching*, Louisville, KY: Westminster John Knox Press.

Long, Thomas G. (2016), *The Witness of Preaching*, Louisville, KY: Westminster John Knox Press.

Marriage in Church After Divorce Form and Explanatory Statement (2003), London: Church House Publishing.

McArdle, Kate Louise (2008), 'Getting in, getting on, getting out: on working with second-person inquiry groups', in Peter Reason and Hilary Bradbury (eds), *The SAGE Handbook of Action Research: Participative Inquiry and Practice* (pp. 602–14), Los Angeles, CA; London; New Delhi; Singapore: Sage.

McNiff, Jean (2014), *Writing and Doing Action Research*, London: Sage.

McNiff, Jean and Whitehead, Jack (2009), *Doing and Writing Action Research*, London: Sage.

Melbourne (2013), Account of the Melbourne co-operative inquiry group, www.dropbox.com/s/071rpop3code1qo/Melbourne.pdf.

Melchert, Charles F. (1998), *Wise Teaching: Biblical Wisdom and Educational Ministry*, Harrisburg, PA: Trinity Press International.

Midgley, Mary (2003), *The Myths We Live By* (pp. 26–7), London: Routledge.

Miller-McLemore, Bonnie J. (ed.) (2012), *The Wiley-Blackwell Companion to Practical Theology*, Malden, MA: Wiley-Blackwell.

Miller, Nod (2000), 'Learning from experience in adult education', in Arthur L. Wilson, Elisabeth R. Hayes and Washington D.C. American Association for Adult

Continuing Education (eds), *Handbook of Adult and Continuing Education* (new edn, pp. 71–86), San Francisco, CA: Jossey-Bass.

Miner, Maureen, Dowson, Martin and Devenish, Stuart (2012), *Beyond Well-being: Spirituality and Human Flourishing*, North Carolina, NC: Information Age Publishing.

Moon, Jennifer A. (2004), *A Handbook of Reflective and Experiential Learning: Theory and Practice*, London: RoutledgeFalmer.

Moore, Andrew (2013), *Preaching – with Integrity*, Cambridge: Grove Books Ltd.

Moschella, Mary Clark (2012), 'Ethnography', in Bonnie J. Miller-McLemore (ed.), *The Wiley-Blackwell Companion to Practical Theology* (pp. 224–33), Malden, MA: Wiley-Blackwell.

Napier, Rodney and Gershenfeld, Matti K. (1999), *Groups: Theory and Experience* (6th edn), Boston, MA: Houghton Mifflin.

New Zealand, Education for Ministry (2013), 'Theological Reflection', retrieved 12 March 2013, www.efm.org.nz/reflections/methods_of_tr.htm.

Olney, James (1981), *Metaphors of Self: The Meaning of Autobiography*, Princeton, NJ: Princeton University Press.

Osmer, Richard Robert (2008), *Practical Theology: An Introduction*, Grand Rapids, MI: Wm. B. Eerdmans Co.

Pattison, Stephen (1989), 'Some straw for the bricks: a basic introduction to theological reflection', *Contact*, 99 (pp. 2–9).

Pattison, Stephen (2000), 'Some straw for the bricks: a basic introduction to theological reflection', in James Woodward, Stephen Pattison and John Patton (eds), *Blackwell Reader in Pastoral and Practical Theology* (pp. 135–45), Malden, MA: Blackwell Publishers.

Pattison, Stephen, Thompson, Judith and Green, John (2003), 'Theological reflection for the real world: time to think again', *British Journal of Theological Education*, 13.2 (pp. 119–31).

Paver, John E. (2006), *Theological Reflection and Education for Ministry: Explorations in Practical, Pastoral and Empirical Theology*, Aldershot: Ashgate.

Ponterotto, Joseph G. (2006), 'Brief note on the origins, evolution, and meaning of the qualitative research concept "thick description"', *The Qualitative Report*, 11(3) (pp. 538–49).

Pratt, Daniel D. and Nesbit, Tom (2000), 'Discourses and cultures of teaching', in Arthur L. Wilson, Elisabeth Hayes and American Association for Adult and Continuing Education (eds) (pp. 117–31), San Francisco, CA: Jossey-Bass.

Reader, John (2005), *Blurred Encounters: A Reasoned Practice of Faith*, St Brides Major: Aureus.

Reason, Peter (2002), 'Introduction: the practice of co-operative inquiry', *Systemic Practice and Action Research*, 15(3) (pp. 169–76).

Reason, Peter and Bradbury, Hilary (eds) (2008), *The Sage Handbook of Action Research: Participative Inquiry and Practice* (2nd edn), Los Angeles, CA; London; New Delhi; Singapore: Sage.

Reinharz, Shulamit (1983), 'Experiential analysis: a contribution to feminist research', in Gloria Bowles and Renate Klein (eds), *Theories of Women's Studies*, London; Boston: Routledge & Kegan Paul.

Richardson, Laurel (2001), 'Getting personal: writing-stories', *International Journal of Qualitative Studies in Education*, 14.1 (pp. 33–8).

Ricoeur, Paul (2008), 'On interpretation', in *From Text to Action: Essays in Hermeneutics II* (p. 9), London: Continuum.

Roncace, Mark and Gray, Patrick (2012), *Teaching the Bible: Practical Strategies for Classroom Instruction* (Vol. 49), New York: Society of Biblical Literature.

Rothwell, Emma (2013), 'Broken silence: researching with women to find a voice', in Slee, Nicola, Porter, Fran and Phillips, Anne (eds), *The Faith Lives of Women and Girls: Qualitative Research Perspectives*, Farnham, Surrey; Burlington, VT: Ashgate.

Royal, Te Ahukaramū Charles (4 March 2009), 'Māori creation traditions – common threads in creation stories', retrieved 28 January 2013, www.teara.govt.nz/en/maori-creation-traditions/1/1.

Rudd, Andrew (2017), 'Sustaining Joy', unpublished poem.

Schön, Donald A. (1983), *The Reflective Practitioner: How Professionals Think in Action*, Aldershot: Avebury.

Segundo, Juan Luis (1977), *Liberation of Theology*, Dublin: Gill & Macmillan Ltd.

Sewanee (2013), 'Account of the Sewanee co-operative inquiry group', www.dropbox.com/s/ida1a3yxfhuvor3/Sewanee.pdf?dl=0.

Shercliff, Liz (2014), 'Do women preach with a different voice?', *The Preacher*, 154, Journal of the College of Preachers.

The Shorter Oxford English Dictionary, Vol. 2 (1972) (3rd 1983 edn), Oxford: Clarendon Press.

Slee, Nicola (2004), *Women's Faith Development: Patterns and Processes*, Aldershot: Ashgate.

Slee, Nicola, Porter, Fran and Phillips, Anne (2013), *The Faith Lives of Women and Girls: Qualitative Research Perspectives*, Farnham, Surrey; Burlington, VT: Ashgate.

Smith, Graeme (2008), 'Something that can be learnt but not taught: teaching theological reflection through enquiry-based learning', *Journal of Adult Theological Education*, 5.1 (pp. 20–3).

Streck, Valburga Schmiedt (2012), 'Brazil', in Bonnie J. Miller-McLemore (ed.), *The Wiley-Blackwell Companion to Practical Theology* (pp. 525–33), Malden, MA: Wiley-Blackwell.

Stringer, Ernest T. (2007), *Action Research* (3rd edn), Los Angeles, CA; London: Sage.

Sweet, Leonard (2014), *Giving Blood: A Fresh Paradigm for Preaching*, Grand Rapids, MI: Zondervan.

Swinton, John and Mowat, Harriet (2006), *Practical Theology and Qualitative Research*, London: SCM Press.

Swinton, John and Mowat, Harriet (2016), *Practical Theology and Qualitative Research* (2nd edn), London: SCM Press.

Tanner, Kathryn (1997), *Theories of Culture: A New Agenda for Theology*, Minneapolis, MN: Fortress Press.

Taylor, Barbara Brown (2013), *The Preaching Life* (2nd edn), Norwich: Canterbury Press.

Taylor, Barbara Brown (2014), *Learning to Walk in the Dark*, Norwich: Canterbury Press.

Thomas, R. S. (1993), 'Pilgrimages', in *Collected Poems 1945–1990*, London: J. M. Dent.

Thompson, Judith, Pattison, Stephen and Thompson, Ross (2008), *SCM Studyguide to Theological Reflection*, London: SCM Press.

Tillich, Paul (1951), *Systematic Theology* (Vol. 1), Chicago: University of Chicago Press.

Tillich, Paul (1959), *Theology of Culture*, New York: Oxford University Press.

Torbert, William R. (1998), 'Developing wisdom and courage in organizing and sciencing', in Suresh Srivastva and David L. Cooperrider (eds), *Organizational Wisdom and Executive Courage* (1st edn), San Francisco, CA: New Lexington Press.

Torbert, William R. and Taylor, Steven S. (2008), 'Action inquiry: interweaving multiple qualities of attention for timely action', in Peter Reason and Hilary Bradbury (eds), *The SAGE Handbook of Action Research: Participative Inquiry and Practice* (2nd edn, pp. 239–51), Los Angeles, CA; London; New Delhi; Singapore: Sage.

Tracy, David (1975), *Blessed Rage for Order, the New Pluralism in Theology*, New York: Seabury Press.

Veling, Terry A. (2005), *Practical Theology: 'On Earth as it is in Heaven'*, Maryknoll, NY: Orbis Books.

von Allmen, Jean-Jacques (1962), *Preaching and Congregation*, Louisville, KY: John Knox Press.

Vygotsky, L. S. (1962), *Thought and Language*, Massachusetts Institute of Technology; Wiley.

Walton, Heather (2014), *Writing Methods in Theological Reflection*, London: SCM Press.

Walton, Roger L. (2002), *The Teaching and Learning of Theological Reflection: Case Studies of Practice*, University of Durham (Available for download at http://ethos.bl.uk/OrderDetails.do?did=8&uin=uk.bl.ethos.403336), unpublished PhD thesis.

Ward, Pete (2017), *Introducing Practical Theology: Mission, Ministry, and the Life of the Church*, Grand Rapids, MI: Baker Academic.

Warren, Heather A., Murray, Joan L. and Best, Mildred M. (2002), 'The discipline and habit of theological reflection', *Journal of Religion and Health*, 41(4) (pp. 323–31).

Watt, Nicholas (November 2014) www.theguardian.com/politics/2014/nov/04/norman-baker-constant-battle-theresa-may-home-office, accessed 5 November 2014.

Whitehead, James D. and Whitehead, Evelyn Eaton (1980), *Method in Ministry: Theological Reflection and Christian Ministry*, New York: Seabury Press.

Whitehead, James D. and Whitehead, Evelyn Eaton (1995), *Method in Ministry: Theological Reflection and Christian Ministry* (revd and updated edn), Kansas City, MO: Sheed & Ward.

Wijsen, Frans Jozef Servaas, Henriot, Peter J. and Mejía, Rodrigo (eds) (2005), *The Pastoral Circle Revisited: A Critical Quest for Truth and Transformation*, Maryknoll, NY: Orbis Books.

Williams, Rowan (1999), *On Christian Theology (Challenges in Contemporary Theology)*, New Jersey, NJ: Wiley-Blackwell.

Williams, Rowan (2000), *Lost Icons: Reflections on Cultural Bereavement*, Edinburgh: T & T Clark.

Wilson, Arthur L., Hayes, Elisabeth and American Association for Adult and Continuing Education (2000), *Handbook of Adult and Continuing Education* (new edn), San Francisco, CA: Jossey-Bass.

Winter, Richard and Munn-Giddings, Carol (eds) (2001), *A Handbook for Action Research in Health and Social Care*, London; New York: Routledge.

Woodward, James, Pattison, Stephen and Patton, John (1999), *The Blackwell Reader in Pastoral and Practical Theology*, Oxford; Malden, MA: Blackwell Publishers.

Yaghjian, Lucretia B. (2006), *Writing Theology Well: A Rhetoric for Theological and Biblical Writers*, New York: Continuum.

Yorks, Lyle, Aprill, Arnold, James, LaDon, Rees, Anita M., Hofman-Pinilla, Amparo and Ospina, Sonia (2008), 'The tapestry of leadership: lessons from six co-operative-inquiry groups of social justice leaders', in Peter Reason and Hilary Bradbury (eds), *The SAGE Handbook of Action Research: Participative Inquiry and Practice* (2nd edn, pp. 487–96), Los Angeles, CA; London; New Delhi; Singapore: Sage.

Index of Biblical References

Index of Names and Subjects